Nǐ Hǎo

③

Chinese Language Course
Intermediate Level

by

Shumang Fredlein • Paul Fredlein

ChinaSoft

(Language Lab software downloadable)

Nǐ Hǎo 3 – Chinese Language Course – Intermediate Level
First published 1995; reprinted 1996, 1997, 1998, 1999, 2000
Revised edition 2003, 2005, 2007
Third edition 2009

ChinaSoft Pty Ltd   ABN: 61 083 458 459
P.O. Box 845, Toowong, Brisbane, Qld 4066, AUSTRALIA
Telephone   (61-7) 3371-7436
Facsimile   (61-7) 3371-6711
www.chinasoft.com.au

Written by Shumang Fredlein (林淑滿) & Paul Fredlein
Cover by Zhengdong Su (苏正东)
Illustrations by Zhengdong Su (苏正东) & Xiaolin Xue (薛晓林)
Software by Paul Fredlein
Edited by Christine Ko, Jemma Fredlein, Linda Smith (陳亮吟)

Printed in Taiwan

Companion Workbook, audio CDs and Games software are also available.

ISBN 978 1 876739 54 6

Preface

你好 Nǐ Hǎo is a basic course for beginning students of Chinese. It introduces Chinese language and culture and aims to teach communication in both spoken and written Chinese. The objectives are to enable students to use Chinese in the classroom, playground, local community and countries where the language is spoken.

The text is richly illustrated for stimulating learning. Characters are used throughout the text to enhance reading and writing ability. Pinyin only acts as a guide to pronunciation. As learning progresses, the Pinyin of the characters that have been learnt is omitted. Various print fonts are used to equip students to read authentic materials. Kǎishū [楷书], used in the main text, is an ideal font to learn to write; Sòngtǐ [宋体], used in the sentence patterns, is a font commonly used in newspapers and general publications; Hēitǐ [黑体], used in titles, is also a common font in publications. Handwritten scripts in cartoons provide students with the opportunity to read handwriting. As traditional characters are used in Taiwan and overseas Chinese communities, the traditional form is included in the vocabulary list in Appendix 1 as reference. (For those who wish to learn traditional characters, the traditional character edition is published by Cheng & Tsui Company in the USA under licence from ChinaSoft.)

There are subsections in each lesson. The *Illustrated texts* sections demonstrate typical conversations in daily life and the illustrations are ideal tools for role playing. The *Learn the sentences* sections provide example sentences which can be used to hold conversations. The *New words and expressions* sections explain the meaning of individual characters to help understand the structure of the word. The *Write the characters* sections illustrate the stroke order to ensure that characters are written correctly. The *Something to know* sections introduce related culture to enrich cultural understanding and to generate interest in learning the language.

Cartoons, jokes, riddles and little stories also play important roles in the book. They are light and cheerful materials offering wonderful opportunities for practice and reinforcement.

This third edition delivers a smooth progression from Ni Hao 2 to Ni Hao 3. Useful language is functionally repeated. More interesting items are added to reinforce learning. Our aim is to ensure that the langugue learnt is useful and that the learning process is effective as well as enjoyable, ensuring fruitful learning outcomes.

Shumang, 2009

Contents

dì yī kè wǒ de kè yè
第一课 我的课业 (My studies)

(1) What subjects do you have? (2) I hate math (3) How did you do in the test?

dì èr kè xué xiào shēng huó
第二课 学校生活 (School life)

(1) Which class are you in? (2) How long have you studied Chinese?
(3) Can I borrow your book? (4) When is the homework due?

dì sān kè zěn me zǒu
第三课 怎么走 (How to get to)

(1) Do you walk to school? (2) Where do you live? (3) How do I get there?

dì sì kè xiū xián shēng huó
第四课 休闲生活 (Leisure life)

(1) What's good on TV? (2) Two movie tickets (3) Busy weekends

dì wǔ kè fù xí
第五课 复习（一）(Revision I)

(1) Letter to a friend (2) Letter to a relative
(3) A little note (4) Language functions

N

黑龙江省 Heilongjiang Prov.
哈尔滨 Harbin
吉林省 Jilin Prov.
辽宁省 Liaoning Prov.
沈阳 Shenyang
长城 The Great Wall (Chang Cheng)
内蒙古自治区 Inner Mongolia Autonomous Region
古
蒙
内
北京 Beijing
天津 Tianjin
河北省 Hebei Prov.
大同 Datong
山西省 Shanxi Prov.
太原 Taiyuan
黄 河 Huang He
山东省 Shandong Prov.
青岛 Qingdao
泰山 Mt Tai
开封 Kaifeng
河南省 Henan Prov.
江苏省 Jiangsu Prov.
扬州 Yangzhou
南京 Nanjing
上海 Shanghai
苏州 Suzhou
安徽省 Anhui Prov.
杭州 Hangzhou
浙江省 Zhejiang Prov.
黄山 Mt Huang
台北 Taibei (Taipei)
台湾 Taiwan
福州 Fuzhou
福建省 Fujian Prov.
厦门 Xiamen
广州 Guangzhou
香港 Hong Kong (Xianggang)
西安 Xi'an
陕 西 省 Shaanxi Prov.
华山 Mt Hua
湖北省 Hubei Prov.
武汉 Wuhan
庐山 Mt Lu
江西省 Jiangxi Prov.
长沙 Changsha
湖南省 Hunan Prov.
桂林 Guilin
广东省 Guangdong Prov.
南宁 Nanning
广西壮族自治区 Guangxi Zhuang Autonomous Region
宁夏回族自治区 Ningxia Hui Autonomous Region
甘肃省 Gansu Prov.
兰州 Lanzhou
成都 Chengdu
四川省 Sichuan Prov.
长 江 Chang Jiang
重庆 Chongqing
贵州省 Guizhou Prov.
昆明 Kunming
新疆维吾尔自治区 Xinjiang Uygur Autonomous Region
乌鲁木齐 Urumqi
敦煌 Dunhuang
青海省 Qinghai Prov.
拉萨 Lhasa
西藏自治区 Xizang (Tibet) Autonomous Region
珠穆朗玛峰 Mt Qomolangma (Mt Everest)
云南省 Yunnan Prov.
海南省 Hainan Prov.

中 国 地 图
Map of China

公里 km
0 100 200 300 400 500

第一课　我的课业

dì yī kè　wǒ de kè yè

1 **What subjects do you have?**

2 I hate math

兰兰，你下一节是体育（tǐ yù），对吧？

对啊（a）！你怎么知道？

我猜（cāi）的。

你上一节是美术（měi shù），对吧？

对啊（a）！你怎么知道？

我也是猜（cāi）的。

你下一节是什么课？

我下一节是数学。唉（ài）！
我最讨厌上数学课了。

唉（ài）！我最讨厌上体育（tǐ yù）课了。

你为什么讨厌上体育课？

因为我没有运动细胞。

谁说你没有运动细胞？
你乒乓球打得很好啊！

我就是讨厌上体育课。

你为什么讨厌上数学课？

因为我没有数学头脑。

谁说你没有数学头脑？你很聪明啊！

我就是讨厌上数学课。

3 **How did you do in the test?**

chéng biǎo 课程表	星期一	星期二	星期三	星期四	星期五
第一节	英语	科学	英语	汉语	科学
第二节	数学	英语	数学	汉语	科学
第三节	数学	英语	数学	地理	地理
第四节	地理	历史	地理	英语	历史
第五节	地理	汉语	音乐	科学	历史
第六节	体育	美术	体育	科学	汉语
第七节	历史	美术	体育	数学	汉语

xìng míng 姓名：黄明汉　　bān 班级：10-3

什么考试？

 **Learn the sentences**

※ **Asking what subjects someone has**

To ask What subjects do you have today? say 你今天有什么课？ To answer, replace 什么课 with the subjects.

你今天有什么课？	我今天有科学、数学和美^{měi shù}术。
他明天有什么课？	他明天有英语、汉语和音^{yīn yuè}乐。
你星期四有什么课？	我星期四有历^{lì shǐ}史、地^{dì lǐ}理和体^{tǐ yù}育。

Note: pinyin annotations appear above the following characters: 美术 (měi shù), 音乐 (yīn yuè), 历史 (lì shǐ), 地理 (dì lǐ), 体育 (tǐ yù).

※ **Asking the subject of a period**

To state a period of the day, use 第一节 for the first period, 第二节 for the second period, or 上一节 for the previous period and 下一节 for the next period. To ask What subject do you have in period two? say 你第二节是什么课？ To answer, replace 什么课 with the subject.

你第二节是什么课？	我第二节是汉语。
你第五节是什么课？	我第五节是科学。
你上一节是什么课？	我上一节是数学。
她下一节是什么课？	她下一节是英语。

Something about Pinyin

In 你好 1 and 你好 2, Pinyin is placed on top of the word. In 你好 3, it is placed on top of each individual character. This is to minimize the dependency on Pinyin for characters that have been learned. In 你好 2, we also learned that sometimes a character in a word is said in a neutral tone, rather than its original tone. In this case, the pinyin is displayed in its original tone in 你好 3 for easy learning, but marked with a blue dot to remind you to say it in a neutral tone. e.g. 衣^{yī}服^{fú·}

✳ Asking for a reason

To ask for a reason, use 为什么, why. To answer, use 因为, because followed by the reason.

你为什么不喜欢上学？	因为我讨厌上体育课？
你为什么讨厌上体育课？	因为我不会游泳。
你为什么不会游泳？	因为我没有运动细胞。
你为什么没有运动细胞？	因为我爸爸没有运动细胞。

✳ Describing one's talent

When describing someone's talent, 头脑 tóunǎo, brain, is used for someone good at science and math, and 细胞 xìbāo, cell, is used for someone good at arts, music and sports.

他哥哥很有数学头脑。	他姐姐很有音乐细胞。
我爸爸没有科学头脑。	我妹妹没有运动细胞。

✳ Asking how someone did in a test

To ask How was your math test? say 你数学考得怎么样？ To answer, replace 怎么样 with the degree of the outcome.

你数学考得怎么样？	我数学考得很差。
你英语考得怎么样？	我英语考得不好。
你地理考得怎么样？	我考得还可以。
你历史考得怎么样？	我考得不错。
你科学考得怎么样？	我考得很好。

✳ **Asking the marks of a test**

To ask the marks of a test, use 得了多少分. The 得 dé here means receive or get. To answer, replace 多少 with the marks.

你汉语得了多少分？	我得了七十五分。
妹妹美术得了多少分？ *měi shù*	她得了九十八分。
他英语考试得了多少分？	他得了六十分。
弟弟昨天的数学考试得了多少分？	他只得了四十六分。

✳ **Asking if someone is prepared for an exam**

To ask Are you prepared for tomorrow's exam? say 明天的考试，你准备了吗？ To answer yes, say 准备了; for no, say 还没.

明天的汉语考试，你准备了吗？ *zhǔn bèi*	我准备了。
下个星期的考试，你准备了吗？	我还没准备。
明天的科学考试，你准备了吗？	还没。我今天晚上得开夜车了。 *kāi yè*
下午的英语考试，你准备了吗？	英语考试？我们下午有英语考试吗？

New words and expressions

1	课业	kèyè	*n.* study, curriculum
	课	kè	*n.* subject, lesson
	数学	shùxué	*n.* mathematics　数 - numbers; 学 - to study, to learn
	科学	kēxué	*n.* science　科 - science; 学 - to study, to learn
	体育	tǐyù	*n.* physical education, sports　体 - body; 育 - education
	猜	cāi	*v.* guess
	地理	dìlǐ	*n.* geography　地 - land, ground; 理 - logic

| 历史 | lìshǐ | *n.* history 历 - experience; 史 - history |
| 美术 | měishù | *n.* the fine arts, art 美 - beautiful; 术 - art, technique |

2

下	xià	*adj.* next; under
节	jié	*m.w.* [for lessons] section, period; *n.* festival
怎么	zěnme	*pro.* how, why
上	shàng	*adj.* previous; upper, e.g. 上一节 - previous lesson
		v. attend, go to, e.g. 上数学课 - attend math lesson
唉	ài	*exclaim.* (a sigh)
讨厌	tǎoyàn	*v.* hate 讨 - to incur; 厌 - to detest
上课	shàngkè	*v.* attend lesson, go to class
为什么	wèishénme	*adv.* why
细胞	xìbāo	*n.* cell (biological)
就是	jiùshì	*adv.* just, simply (emphasizing a fact) 就 - merely; then, therefore
头脑	tóunǎo	*n.* brain 头 - head; 脑 - brain
聪明	cōngmíng	*adj.* clever 聪 - clever; 明 - bright

3

考试	kǎoshì	*n.* examination, test; *v.* take/give test 试 - test, to try
考	kǎo	*v.* take/give an examination or a test
还可以	hái kěyǐ	*colloq.* not bad, OK
差	chà	*adj.* not good, not up to standard
得	de	[used after a verb to indicate degree], e.g. 考得很好 - did the test very well
	dé	*v.* receive, get, e.g. 得十分 - received 10 marks
	děi	*v.* have to, must
分	fēn	*n.* mark; minute; cent
只	zhǐ	*adv.* only; [zhī- measure word for dogs, birds etc.]
准备	zhǔnbèi	*v.* prepare 准 - standard; 备 - to prepare
开夜车	kāi yèchē	*v.* study or work late into the night 开 - to drive; 夜车 - night train
好好儿	hǎohāor	*adv.* to one's best (The second 好 is said as first tone when followed by a 儿), aslo said as 好好 hǎohǎo

:)

课程表	kèchéng biǎo	*n.* school timetable 课程 - curriculum; 表 - chart
姓名	xìngmíng	*n.* full name 姓 - surname; 名 - name
班级	bānjí	*n.* class and grade 班 - class; 级 - grade

就是知道

你讨厌上数学课。

对，我讨厌上数学课！

měi shù
你喜欢上美术课。

我是喜欢上美术课！

chàng gē
你唱歌唱得不好。

yīn yuè xì bāo
因为我爸爸没有
音乐细胞！

yóu yǒng
你游泳也游得不好。

xì bāo
因为我妈妈没有
运动细胞！

yóu yǒng
你哥哥游泳游得不错。

tóu nǎo
可是他没有
科学头脑！

chàng gē
你妹妹唱歌唱得不错。

tóu nǎo
可是她没有
数学头脑！

你昨天的科学考试考得
很差。

对，我只得了
四十三分。

yīn yuè
你明天第二节是音乐。

没错！我第二节是音乐。

你明天第五节有数学考试。

a
啊！我明天有
数学考试！

你都还没准备。

wàng
我忘了有考试！

kāi yè
你今天晚上得开夜车。

你怎么都知道？

我就是知道。

✏️ Write the characters

第 dì *(order)*	课 kè *lesson, subject*	数 shù *numbers*	科 kē *science*	知 zhī *to know*
道 dào *way*	节 jié *section; festival*	讨 tǎo *to incur*	厌 yàn *to detest*	就 jiù *merely; then, therefore*
考 kǎo *to take/give a test*	试 shì *test, to try*	差 chà *not good*	准 zhǔn *standard*	备 bèi *to prepare*

Dongdong's schoolwork · Dongdong's schoolwork · Dongdong's schoolwork · Dongdong's schoolwork

冬冬

冬冬姓黄，名冬平。因为他喜欢冬天，所以大家都叫他冬冬。
冬冬今天有英语、数学、地理、音乐和体育。冬冬很讨厌上体
育课，因为他不会游泳。冬冬喜欢数学。他的数学考试都考得
很好。大家都说，冬冬有数学头脑，可是没有运动细胞。

Dongdong's schoolwork · Dongdong's schoolwork · Dongdong's schoolwork · Dongdong's schoolwork

Something to know

❀ School subjects

Chinese high school students study common subjects such as Chinese, math and foreign languages until year eleven when they choose to focus on either science or arts according to their future study plans. Those who choose science have a heavier focus on physics, chemistry and biology, whereas those who choose arts have a heavier focus on history, geography and politics. The past few years has seen a trend in changing this division to allow students a wider choice of cross-discipline study.

❀ Chinese painting

The art of Chinese painting is related to the art of calligraphy. The tools for painting are the calligraphy brush and ink. As in other civilizations, early paintings were mainly of human activities and animals for the purpose of communication, moral teachings and religious belief. By as early as the 10th century, Chinese painting started serving a more decorative purpose.

Chinese painters are scholars and masters of calligraphy. They liken the natural scenery to their spiritual mind apart from worldly affairs. This aspect is displayed in typical paintings showing people in very small scale doing activities within a massive mountain and river landscape. This type of painting is called 山水画 shānshuǐ huà, mountain-water painting. Two other popular types of painting are 花鸟画 huāniǎo huà, flower-bird painting, and 人物画 rénwù huà, character painting. Two styles, impressionistic

and realistic, are created using distinctive Chinese brush techniques. The former uses simple and few lines, as in the grass style 草书 cǎoshū in calligraphy, while the latter uses complex and detailed lines.

Unlike traditional western painting that uses a harder brush and shading to create three-dimensional realistic imagery, Chinese painting is plain in layout. Poems or the painter's notations are often inscribed. Paintings are on paper or silk and are mounted onto a scroll, which can be either rolled up for storage or unrolled for hanging. Very long scrolls are unrolled horizontally for viewing.

An artist's re-creation of "Walking with a Stick" by Shen Zhou (1427-1509). The small scale of the person is characteristic of the mountain-water painting.

1 Which class are you in?

2 How long have you studied Chinese?

3 Can I borrow your book?

4 When is the homework due?

Learn the sentences

❋ **Stating the grade and class**

To state the grade and class someone is in, use x 年级 x 班, for example, 十一年级七班, grade eleven and class seven.

你在几年级几班？	我在十一年级七班。
你哥哥在几年级几班？	他在十二年级五班。
你妹妹在几班？	她在四年级六班。

❋ **Asking which school someone attends**

To ask Which school do you go to? say 你上哪个学校？ To answer, replace 哪个学校 with the name of the school.

你上哪个学校？	我上第九中学。
你弟弟上哪个学校？	他上男子文法学校。
你妹妹上哪个学校？	她上中山女子中学。
你以前上哪个学校？	我以前上中山男子中学。

❋ **Asking the number of students**

To ask How many students are there at your school? say 你们学校有多少学生？ To answer, replace 多少 with the number, for example, 五千多, more than five thousand. The 多 in 多少 in the question carries the meaning of how and in 五千多 which follows a number means more than.

你们学校有多少学生？	我们学校有五千多个学生。
他们学校有多少学生？	他们学校只有五百多个学生。
你们班有多少学生？	我们班有二十五个学生。

※ **Asking how long someone has learned Chinese**

To ask How long have you studied Chinese? say 你学习汉语多久了？ To answer, replace 多久 with the length of time, for example, 两年多, more than two years. The 多 in 多久 carries the meaning of how and in 两年多 means more than.

你学习汉语多久了？	我学习汉语两年多了。
你哥哥学习汉语多久了？	他学习汉语三年了。
你爸爸学习英语多久了？	他学习英语五年多了。

※ **Asking the meaning of a word/sentence**

To ask the meaning of a word or a sentence, use 是什么意思, what does it mean. To answer, use 是 or 就是 followed by its meaning. 就是 is used when emphasizing.

"马马虎虎" 是什么意思？	"马马虎虎" 就是 so so。
"流利" 是什么意思？	"流利" 是 fluent。
"为什么" 是什么意思？	"为什么" 就是 why。

※ **Seeking permission to borrow something**

To ask permission to borrow something, use xx 借我，好吗？ To give definite permission, use 行, or for reluctant permission, use 好吧. To deny permission, say 不行.

汉语字典借我，好吗？	行，拿去吧！
你的英语课本借我，好吗？	好吧！拿去吧！
你的数学作业借我，好吗？	不行，作业不借你。
你的地理课本借我，好吗？	我忘了带地理课本。

＊ **Asking if someone has completed something**

To ask Have you done your homework? say 你作业做了吗？ The 了 used after a verb, i.e. v + 了, indicates the action being completed. To answer yes, say 做了；for no, say 还没 or 还没做.

姐姐作业做了吗？	她做了。
妹妹作业做了吗？	她还没做。
弟弟早饭吃了吗？	他还没吃。
哥哥来了吗？	他还没来。
你作业做了吗？	^{zāo gāo} 糟糕！我忘了做。

＊ **Asking how to say something in Chinese**

To ask How do you say "so so" in Chinese? say "So so" 的汉语怎么说？ To answer, use 是 followed by its meaning in Chinese.

"Pay attention" 的汉语怎么说？	是 "注意听"。 ^{zhù yì tīng}
"So so" 的汉语怎么说？	是 "马马虎虎"。 ^{hū hū}
"I forgot" 的汉语怎么说？	是 "我忘了"。

※ **Asking when to hand in an assignment**

To say hand in the homework/assignment, use 交作业. To ask, When do we need to hand in the assignment? say 我们什么时候要交作业？ To answer, replace 什么时候 with the time.

我们什么时候要交作业？	我们明天要交作业。
姐姐什么时候要交数学作业？	她下个星期要交。
弟弟什么时候要交英语作业？	他昨天要交！！
你什么时候要交汉语作业？	汉语作业？我没有汉语作业。

New words and expressions

1

生活	shēnghuó	*n.* life 生 - to be born; 活 - to live
新	xīn	*adj.* new
班	bān	*n.* class
以前	yǐqián	*adv.* previously, before
女	nǚ	*n.* woman, female
女子中学	nǚzǐ zhōngxué	*n.* girl's middle/high school 女子 - female
哦	ò	*exclaim.* [indicating understanding or realization]
男	nán	*n.* man, male
男女合校	nán nǚ héxiào	*n.* co-educational school 合 - to combine; 校 - school
千	qiān	*n.* thousand
多	duō	*adj.* 1. more than, over, e.g. 两千多 - more than two thousand; 一年多 - more than one year 2. many, much, e.g. 很多 - many/much *adv.* [indicating degree or extent] how, e.g. 多久 - how long (time duration)

2

学习	xuéxí	*v.* study, learn 学 - to study, to learn; 习 - to practise
久	jiǔ	*adj.* long (of time)
流利	liúlì	*adj.* fluent 流 - to flow; 利 - sharp
马马虎虎	mǎmǎ hūhū	*collq.* 1. so-so; 2. careless, casual (so as to not tell the difference between a horse and a tiger) 马 - horse; 虎 hǔ - tiger (said as first tone here)

意思	yìsi	*n.* meaning 意 - meaning; 思 sī - to think

3

课本	kèběn	*n.* textbook 课 - lesson, subject; 本 - *m.w.* book, magazine etc.
借	jiè	*v.* lend; borrow
行	xíng	*v.* OK; to go
拿去	ná qù	*v.* take (away from the speaker); 拿来 - take (towards the speaker)
作业	zuòyè	*n.* school assignment, homework 作 - to do; 业 - course of study
嘘	xū	*colloq.* shh...
说话	shuōhuà	*v.* talk, speak 说 - to speak; 话 - speech
忘	wàng	*v.* forget
向	xiàng	*prep.* to, towards (direction)

4

迟到	chídào	*v.* be late 迟 - late; 到 - to arrive; to go to
睡过头	shuì guò tóu	*v.* sleep in accidentally 睡 - to sleep; 过 - to pass; 头 - head
以后	yǐhòu	*adv.* later, after
可以	kěyǐ	*v.* may, can
嘿	hēi	*exclaim.* hey
糟糕	zāogāo	*exclaim.* oh no; how terrible 糟 - in a wretched stage; 糕 - cake
注意	zhùyì	*v.* pay attention to, take notice of
问题	wèntí	*n.* question, problem 问 - to ask; 题 - topic, subject
交	jiāo	*v.* hand in, e.g. 交作业 - hand in homework

文法学校	wénfǎ xuéxiào	*n.* grammar school 文法 - grammar
男子中学	nánzǐ zhōngxué	*n.* boy's middle/high school 男子 - male

Something about characters

男 man or male, was earlier written as , which represents a strong hand/muscle working in a rice field;

女 woman or female, was earlier written as , which is a picture of a kneeling woman.

为什么?

Write the characters

班 bān class	校 xiào school	女 nǚ woman, female	男 nán man, male	千 qiān thousand
百 bǎi hundred	习 xí to practise	久 jiǔ long (of time)	本 běn [m.w. for books etc.]	作 zuò to do
业 yè course of study	忘 wàng to forget	迟 chí late	到 dào to; to arrive, to go to	交 jiāo to hand in

Dongdong and friends · Dongdong and friends · Dongdong and friends · Dongdong and friends · Dongdong and friends · Dongdong and friends · Dongdong and friends · Dongdong and friends · Dongdong and friends · Dongdong and friends · Dongdong and friends · Dongdong and friends

马马虎虎（hū hū）？

冬冬上明山中学，九年级四班。明山中学不大，只有四百多个学生。冬冬有两个好朋友，一个叫春风，一个叫秋雨。春风常常上课迟到，不注意（zhù yì）听，不交作业，忘了带（dài）课本。秋雨喜欢问（wèn）很多问题（wèn tí）。他常常问（wèn）冬冬，这是什么意思（yì sī），那是什么意思（yì sī）；这个的汉语怎么说，那个的汉语怎么说。秋雨学习汉语一年多了。他的汉语说得很流（liú）利（lì）。他最喜欢说的是"马马虎虎（hū hū）"。

Something to know

❀ Home classroom

As high school students in China and Taiwan do not have many elective subjects, most students stay in their home classroom to study and take their afternoon nap. It is only when they need to use special equipment that they go to the chemistry laboratory, the computer room or the kitchen. Senior students who choose the same field of study, either science or arts, are placed in the same class and share the same home classroom.

❀ Radicals of Chinese characters

Chinese characters consist of one, two or more components. A radical is the basic component of each character and normally relates to the meaning of the character. Some characters are radicals themselves, while some contain a radical and other component(s). In most cases, the other component(s) indicates the sound of the character. Although components may not always be pronounced exactly the same in different characters, there is always some degree of similarity. For example:

Characters that are radicals:

女 nǚ, 言 yán, 口 kǒu, 人 rén, 日 rì

Characters with the same radicals:

好 hǎo, 她 tā, 妈 mā, 姐 jiě, 妹 mèi – radical 女 nǚ, woman
谁 shéi, 谢 xiè, 请 qǐng, 说 shuō, 话 huà, 语 yǔ – radical 讠(言) yán, speech
吗 ma, 吧 ba, 呢 ne, 哪 nǎ, 吃 chī, 喝 hē – radical 口 kǒu, mouth
晴 qíng, 明 míng, 昨 zuó – radical 日 rì, sun

Characters with different radicals but with the same components and similar pronunciation:

妈 mā, 吗 ma – component 马 mǎ
晴 qíng, 请 qǐng – component 青 qīng
作 zuò, 昨 zuó – component 乍 zhà
快 kuài, 块 kuài – component 夬 kuài

The radical and number of strokes are used to find a character in the dictionary whose pronunciation is not known. However, when the pronunciation is known, the quickest way to look up a character is to use the Pinyin alphabetical listing. A list of the radicals is in Appendix 3.

dì　sān　kè　zěn　me　zǒu
第三课　怎么走

1 **Do you walk to school?**

你骑车到学校要多长时间？

我骑车要二十几分钟。

小明坐火车到学校要多长时间？

他坐火车要半个多小时。

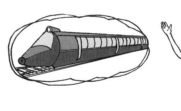

兰兰坐公共汽车到学校要多长时间？

她坐车也要半个多小时。你呢？

你走路到学校要多长时间？

我走路只要十几分钟。

2 **Where do you live?**

李秋，你住在哪里？

我住在东山^{qū}区。

你住在哪里？

我住在西山区。

兰兰住在哪里？

兰兰也住在西山区。

大伟呢？

大伟住在南山区。

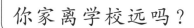

你家离学校远吗？

不远。我家离学校很近，只有两公里。你家离学校远吗？

我家离学校很远，差不多三十公里。

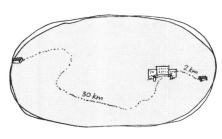

兰兰家离学校远吗？

兰兰家离学校也很远，差不多二十五公里。

大伟呢？

大伟家离学校不远，只有五公里。

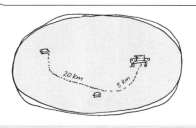

3 How do I get there?

Learn the sentences

✳ Asking the mode of transport

To ask Do you walk to school? say 你走路上学吗？ For a positive answer, say 是的; for a negative answer, say 不.

你走路上学吗？	是的，我天天走路上学。
他坐公共汽车上学吗？	不，他坐火车上学。
你弟弟骑自行车上学吗？	不，他走路上学。

✳ Use of 多 and 几 to state an amount

多 and 几 are often used after a number to add more to that figure. 多 is used to mean over or more than, i.e. 一个多小时 means over one hour. 几 is usually used after values of ten to mean a few, i.e. 二十几 means twenty something.

多:	半个多小时	一个多小时
	一百多个学生	两千多个学生
几:	十几个小时	二十几个小时
	十几分钟 zhōng	四十几分钟

✳ Asking the length of time

To ask about the length of time required, use 多长时间, how long (of time). To answer, state the length of time, for example, 半个多小时, more than half an hour and 五分钟, five minutes.

到那儿要多长时间？	要一个小时。
你走路到学校要多长时间？	要十几分钟。 zhōng
他坐公共汽车到学校要多长时间？	要半个多小时。
骑车到火车站要多长时间？	只要五分钟。 zhōng

✳ Asking where someone lives

To ask Where do you live? say 你住在哪里？ To answer, replace 哪里 with the place name, which can be a district or a city.

你住在哪里？	我住在悉尼。 xī ní
你姐姐住在哪里？	我姐姐住在纽约。 niǔ yuē
你爸爸住在哪里？	我爸爸住在伦敦。 lún dūn

✳ Asking if a place is far away

To ask Is your home far from school? say 你家离学校远吗？ The word 离 lí means away from. To answer, replace 远吗 with 很远, 不远 or 很近. To be more complete, add the distance.

你家离学校远吗？	很远，差不多十五公里。
他家离学校远吗？	他家离学校很远，差不多二十公里。
中国城离这儿远吗？	中国城离这儿不远，只有三公里。
火车站离这儿远吗？	很近，只有一公里。

✳ **Giving directions**

To give directions, 往 wǎng is commonly used which means to, towards, for example, 往前走, walk straight forward; 往右拐, turn to the right. To ask directions, use 怎么走, how to get to.

到火车站怎么走？ 到图书馆怎么走？ tú 到小卖部怎么走？ bù	你往前走，到十字路口往右拐。 guǎi 你往北走，到红绿灯路口往西拐。 dēng 你往右走，过了图书馆往左拐。 tú

十字路口　　　　　红绿灯路口

【你猜是什么？】 cāi

你往前走他也往前走；你往后走他也往后走。

你的左边是他的右边；你的右边是他的左边。

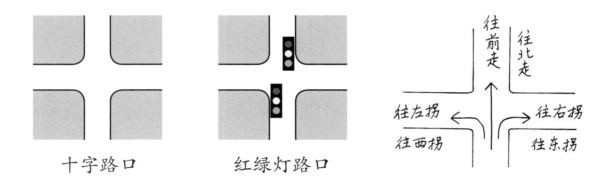

Something about characters

东 east, 東 in the traditional form, was written earlier as 東 , which represents a sun rising behind a tree;

西 west, was earlier written as 囟 , which represents birds sitting in a nest;

走 to walk, was earlier written as 走 , which is a picture of a person walking hurriedly;

行 to go, was earlier written as 彳 , which represents two legs of a person moving along.

没错

你要去邮局^{yóu jú}啊^a？邮局离这儿不远，差不多半公里，走路只要三分钟^{zhōng}。你往前走再往东拐^{guǎi}——不对，那里是火车站。你往前走再往西拐——不对，那里是图书馆^{tú}。你往西走再往南拐——不对，那里是学校。你往东走再往北拐。没错，邮局^{yóu jú}就在马路的右边。

New words and expressions

1	走	zǒu	*v.* walk, go
	走路	zǒulù	*v.* walk 走 - to walk, to go; 路 - road
	骑	qí	*v.* ride (bicycle or horse)
	自行车	zìxíngchē	*n.* bicycle, bike 自 - self; 行 - to go; OK; 车 - vehicle, car
	天天	tiāntiān	*n.* every day
	火车	huǒchē	*n.* train 火 - fire; 车 - vehicle, car
	公共汽车	gōnggòng qìchē	*n.* bus 公 - public; 共 - altogether; 汽 - steam; 车 - vehicle, car; 公共 - public; 汽车 - automobile
	到	dào	1. *prep.* to; 2. *v.* arrive, go to
	时间	shíjiān	*n.* time 时 - time, hour; 间 - within
	几	jǐ	*numeral.* a few; how many
	钟	zhōng	*n.* clock, commonly added to 分 or 点 to show the time, e.g. 三分钟 - three minutes; 三点钟 - three o'clock

小时	xiǎoshí	*n.* hour 时 - time, hour

2

住	zhù	*v.* live, reside
东	dōng	*n.* east
区	qū	*n.* area, district
西	xī	*n.* west
南	nán	*n.* south
离	lí	*adv.* away from
远	yuǎn	*adj.* far
近	jìn	*adj.* near, close
公里	gōnglǐ	*n.* kilometer (km)
差不多	chàbuduō	*adv.* approximately, nearly 差 - differ, not good

北

西　　東

南

3

邮局	yóujú	*n.* post office 邮 - post, mail; 局 - bureau
往	wǎng	*prep.* towards, to
十字路口	shízì lùkǒu	*n.* crossroads 十字 - cross; 路口 - intersection
拐	guǎi	*v.* turn
马路	mǎlù	*n.* road, street 马 - horse; 路 - road
站	zhàn	*n.* station; *v.* stand; 火车站 - railway station
红绿灯	hónglǜdēng	*n.* traffic light 红 - red; 绿 - green; 灯 - light
路口	lùkǒu	*n.* intersection, crossing 路 - road; 口 - mouth
劳驾	láojià	[polite word used when asking for help] excuse me; may I trouble you
图书馆	túshūguǎn	*n.* library 图 - picture; 书 - book; 馆 - building
过	guò	*v.* pass, cross
办公室	bàngōngshì	*n.* office 办 - to handle; 公 - public; 室 - room
礼堂	lǐtáng	*n.* assembly hall, auditorium 礼 - ritual, courtesy; 堂 - a hall or room for a special purpose
对面	duìmiàn	*n.* opposite (location) 对 - opposite, correct
小卖部	xiǎomàibù	*n.* tuck shop, canteen 卖 - to sell; 部 - part
教室	jiàoshì	*n.* classroom 教 - to teach; 室 - room
操场	cāochǎng	*n.* sports ground 操 - physical exercise; 场 - field, ground
旁边	pángbian	*n.* the side

:)

悉尼	Xīní	*n.* Sydney, also said as 雪梨 Xuělí
纽约	Niǔyuē	*n.* New York
伦敦	Lúndūn	*n.* London

走很远

嘿！上课了。(hēi)

我知道。

你要去哪里？

去小卖部。(bù)

你不去上课吗？

去啊！我马上去。(a)

你为什么迟到？

因为我得上厕所。(cè)

上厕所要二十分钟吗？(cè)(zhōng)

因为我走很远。

厕所离这儿远吗？(cè)

厕所离这儿不远。

那么，你为什么要走很远？你怎么走？

我上了厕所以后往前走，过了图书馆往左拐，(cè)(tú)(guǎi)
过了礼堂往左拐，(lǐ táng)
过了操场往左拐，(cāo chǎng)
过了办公室往右拐。(bàn shì)

那么，教室在哪里？(jiào shì)

教室在办公室旁边。(bàn)(páng)

没错！也就是厕所后面。(cè)

Write the characters

走 zǒu *to walk, to go*	路 lù *road*	骑 qí *to ride (bicycle or horse)*	自 zì *self*	行 xíng *to go; OK*
坐 zuò *to sit, to board*	火 huǒ *fire*	公 gōng *public*	汽 qì *steam*	长 cháng *long*
住 zhù *to live, to reside*	东 dōng *east*	西 xī *west*	南 nán *south*	离 lí *away from*
远 yuǎn *far*	近 jìn *near, close*	往 wǎng *toward, to*	站 zhàn *station; to stand*	过 guò *to pass, to cross*

and school · Dongdong and school · Dongdong and school · Dongdong and school ·

很近？

冬冬说他家离学校很近，差不多半公里。冬冬不是走路上学；他走路到学校要一个半小时。他也不是骑车上学；他骑车到学校也要一个多小时。冬冬坐公共汽车和火车上学，他到学校要五十几分钟。冬冬说，他游泳到学校只要十分钟。
_{zhōng} _{yóu yǒng} _{zhōng}

Something to know

❀ Daily transport

For the majority of people in China, bicycles and buses are the usual modes of transport. Bicycles are economical and convenient – students ride them to school, workers ride them to work and housewives ride them to the markets. Buses carry people around the city and from town to town in an economical way. Private cars and taxis are luxurious forms of transport for most people, although they are becoming more popular. In the countryside, horse-drawn carts, handcarts and trucks are used for carrying goods, but bicycles are still the most common daily mode of transport for most people.

Taxis are commonly used in Taiwan. Vacant taxis cruise the streets and stop to pick up passengers when hailed. The use of private cars has boomed, particularly in the last two decades. This has contributed greatly to traffic problems. In Taipei, it is difficult to find a parking space and traffic flow is slow in peak hours. A subway system has been recently constructed in Taipei to relieve traffic congestion.

❀ The Silk Road

The Silk Road, named by a German in the 19th century, is the collective name of several routes formed over centuries between China and its neighboring Central Asian countries for the purpose of trade. Traders traveling through these routes to the west had to cross vast deserts and high mountains in harsh weather conditions and risk attacks from bandits. In the Tang Dynasty, a monk called 玄奘 Xuánzàng traveled through one of these dangerous routes to India to collect Buddhist scripts which he translated into Chinese. His adventurous journey was transformed into a popular story called 西游记 Xīyóujì *Journey to the West*, also known as *The Monkey King*. In the story, the monk 唐三藏 Táng Sānzàng was accompanied by three magical pupils; the monkey 孙悟空 Sūn Wùkōng, the pig 猪八戒 Zhū Bājiè and the fish 沙悟净 Shā Wùjìng. Its many exciting adventures have made the story very popular.

Story of 西游记 Xīyóujì

1 **What's good on TV?**

2 Two movie tickets

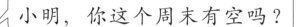

小明，你这个周末有空吗？

有啊！有什么事吗？

请你去看电影，我有两张票。

好啊！是什么电影？

是功夫电影。
gōng fū

我们什么时候去？

我不去，我对功夫电影没兴趣。
gōng fū　　　　xìng qù

你星期六和大伟一块儿去。

3 Busy weekends

你们周末都做什么？

我喜欢热门音乐。我周末常去听音乐会。

这个周末有一场音乐会，我现在去买票。

我对音乐没兴趣。我是球迷，喜欢看

球赛。我周末常去看足球赛和网球赛。

我对球赛没兴趣。我会拉小提琴，也

会弹钢琴。我周末在教钢琴。

我会弹吉他，喜欢古典音乐。我们学校

下个周末有一个中国晚会，请大家来看。

中国晚会

时间：六月十七日，晚上七点到九点

地点：学校礼堂
　　　　dì　　　lǐ táng

节目：舞龙、舞狮、打太极拳、弹古筝、
　　　mù　wǔ lóng　wǔ shī　　　jí quán　tán gǔ zhēng

　　　拉二胡、吹笛子、唱京剧、唱民歌
　　　lā hú　chuī dí　chàng jù　chàng mín gē

门票：免费
mén　miǎn fèi

电视节目　　8月25日　（星期六）	
中国电视台—1（2频道）	北京电视台—1（6频道）
19:35　新闻	9:40　北京中学篮球赛
20:05　电视剧：冬冬的春天	11:20　学英语
21:25　中国音乐	19:30　新闻和天气预报
	20:20　电视剧：他们一家人
中国电视台—2（8频道）	22:55　周末电影
18:35　英语教室	
19:40　美国网球赛	北京电视台—2（21频道）
20:10　京剧：西游记	20:02　动画片：三只小狗
	20:32　中国功夫
中国电视台—3（15频道）	21:05　学京剧
19:30　体育节目	
20:08　电视剧：十字路口	北京有线电视台（24频道）
21:12　新闻	9:00　周末动画片
22:42　古典音乐	21:30　电影：卧虎藏龙

Learn the sentences

✳ **Asking if there is anything good**

To ask for something good, use 有什么好的 or 有什么好 (v.) 的. To answer, state what there is, or if there is nothing, use 没什么好的.

今天有什么好的电视节目？	今天有一场足球比赛。
晚上有什么好的电视节目？	有一部动画片儿，挺有意思的。
明天有什么好的电视节目？	明天没什么好的节目。
今天家里有什么好吃的？	有蛋糕和冰淇淋。

✳ **Use of v + 过 to state past experience**

v + 过 is used to express a past experience, for example 看过, have seen. To ask Have you seen that match? say 那场比赛你看过了吗？ To answer yes, say 看过了; for no, say 还没.

那场比赛你看过了吗？	那场比赛我看过了。
这部动画片儿你看过了吗？	看过了，我看过五次了。
这本书你看过了吗？	还没看过，借我好吗？

✳ Use of 别 + v to give advice

别 + v is used to advise someone not to do something, or stop doing something, for example, 别忘了, don't forget; 别看电视了, stop watching TV. It is usually followed by a 了.

别看电视了，去做^{gōng}功课吧！

别说话了，老师在看你了。

别^{wán}玩^{nǎo}电脑了，去^{shuì jiào}睡觉！

明天别忘了^{dài}带汉语字^{diǎn}典。

✳ Expressing an interest

To express an interest in something, use 对 xx 有兴趣, or for a lack of interest, use 对 xx 没兴趣. The 对 here carries the meaning of towards, i.e. 你对网球比赛有兴趣吗？ literally means Do you have an interest towards tennis matches?.

你对^{wǎng}网球比赛有^{xìng qù}兴趣吗？	有，我是^{wǎng}网球迷。
他对^{huàn}科幻电影有^{xìng qù}兴趣吗？	有，他最喜欢^{huàn}科幻电影了。
你妈妈对^{zú}足球比赛有兴趣吗？	没有，她对球赛没兴趣。
你对^{qí}下棋有兴趣吗？	没有，我对^{qí}下棋没兴趣。

✳ **Use of 迷 to describe a person**

When 迷 mí is attached to a noun, it shows that the person is devoted to that particular thing, for example 电视迷, TV addict; 球迷, ball game fan.

> 弟弟是电视迷；他一天到晚看电视。
>
> 哥哥是足球迷；他天天看足球赛。
>
> 姐姐是电影迷；她看了太多电影了。

New words and expressions

1 休闲	xiūxián	*n.* leisure 休 - to rest; 闲 - leisure
无聊	wúliáo	*adj.* bored, boring 无 - nil, not; 聊 - to chat
节目	jiémù	*n.* program 节 - section; festival; 目 - item; eye
频道	píndào	*n.* (TV or radio) channel 频 - frequency; 道 - road, way
部	bù	*m.w.* [for films, cars etc.]; *n.* part
电视剧	diànshìjù	*n.* television drama 电视 - television; 剧 - play, drama
意思	yìsi	*n.* 1. fun, e.g. 有意思 - interesting, 没意思 - not interesting; 2. meaning 意 - meaning; 思 sī - to think
场	chǎng	*m.w.* [for shows, ball games etc.]; field, ground
比赛	bǐsài	*n.* match, contest 比 - to compare; 赛 - match, contest
过	guò	*par.* [indicating a past experience]; *v.* pass, cross
动画片儿	dònghuàpiānr	*n.* cartoon, also said as 动画片 dònghuàpiàn, or 卡通片 kǎtōngpiàn 画 - picture, painting
次	cì	*m.w.* [for frequency] time
新闻	xīnwén	*n.* news 新 - new; 闻 - to hear, to smell
搞错	gǎocuò	*v.* make mistake, e.g. 你有没有搞错？ - Are you out of your mind?
一天到晚	yìtiān-dàowǎn	*adv.* all day long, from morning till night
迷	mí	*n.* enthusiast, fan, e.g. 电视迷 diànshìmí - television addict, 球迷 qiúmí - ball game fan
2 周末	zhōumò	*n.* weekend 周 - week; 末 - end
电影	diànyǐng	*n.* movie 电 - electricity; 影 - movie, shadow
张	zhāng	*m.w.* [for ticket, paper etc.]; *n.* Zhāng - a surname

票	piào	*n.* ticket
功夫	gōngfū	*n.* kung fu, Chinese martial arts
对	duì	*prep.* towards, to (regarding an attitude); *adj.* correct, right
兴趣	xìngqù	*n.* interest (in something)
科幻	kēhuàn	*n.* science fiction 科 (学)- science; 幻 (想)- fiction

3

热门	rèmén	*n.* popular, e.g. 热门音乐 rèmén yīnyuè - pop music
音乐会	yīnyuè huì	*n.* concert 音乐 - music; 会 - gathering
球迷	qiúmí	*n.* ball game fan 球 - ball; 迷 - fan
球赛	qiúsài	*n.* ball game, match 球 - ball; 赛 - match, contest
赛	sài	*n.* match, contest
拉	lā	*v.* play (violin, erhu etc.); pull
小提琴	xiǎotíqín	*n.* violin 提 - to carry; 琴 - stringed instrument
弹	tán	*v.* play (piano, guitar, guzheng etc.); spring, flick
钢琴	gāngqín	*n.* piano 钢 - steel; 琴 - stringed instrument
教	jiāo	*v.* teach
吉他	jítā	*n.* guitar
古典	gǔdiǎn	*adj.* classical, e.g. 古典音乐 gǔdiǎn yīnyuè - classical music
晚会	wǎnhuì	*n.* evening entertainment 晚 - evening; 会 - gathering

☺

地点	dìdiǎn	*n.* place 地 - land, ground; 点 - o'clock; dot
舞龙	wǔlóng	*n.* dragon dance 舞 - dance, to dance; 龙 - dragon
舞狮	wǔshī	*n.* lion dance 舞 - dance, to dance; 狮 - lion
古筝	gǔzhēng	*n.* a 21- or 25-stringed plucked instrument
二胡	èrhú	*n.* a two-stringed instrument played with a bow
吹	chuī	*v.* play (flute, recorder etc.); blow
笛子	dízi	*n.* flute
唱	chàng	*v.* sing
京剧	jīngjù	*n.* Peking opera (北)京 - Beijing; 剧 - play, drama
民歌	míngē	*n.* folk song, also called 民谣 mínyáo 民 - civilian; 歌 - song; 谣 - ballad
门票	ménpiào	*n.* entrance ticket 门 - door, gate; 票 - ticket
免费	miǎnfèi	*v.* free of charge
电视台	diànshìtái	*n.* television station
西游记	Xīyóujì	*n.* Journey to the West, a Chinese classical novel telling the story of the Monkey King
有线电视	yǒuxiàn diànshì	*n.* cable TV 线 - line, thread
卧虎藏龙	Wòhǔ Cánglóng	*n.* Crouching Tiger, Hidden Dragon, a popular Chinese kung fu movie 卧 - to crouch, to lie down; 藏 - to hide

兴趣

你星期四有空吗？我请
你去看这部功夫电影。

那部功夫电影我看过了。

那么，我请你星期五
去看这部科幻电影。

那部科幻电影
很没意思。

spaceman

那么，我请你周末去看足球赛。

对不起，我对
足球赛没兴趣。

那么，我请你去看板球赛怎么样？

对不起，我对板球赛
也没有兴趣。

那么，你喜欢音乐吗？今天晚上有一场音乐会。

今天晚上这场音乐会？太好了，你买
三张票。我带我的男朋友一块儿去。

Write the characters

视 shì *sight, to look at*	部 bù *[m.w. for films]; part*	意 yì *meaning*	思 sī *to think*	场 chǎng *[m.w. for shows]; field*
比 bǐ *to compare*	赛 sài *match, contest*	别 bié *don't*	迷 mí *fan; to lose one's way*	周 zhōu *week*
末 mò *end*	影 yǐng *movie, shadow*	张 zhāng; Zhāng *[m.w. for paper]; a surname*	票 piào *ticket*	音 yīn *sound*

Dongdong and TV • Dongdong and TV • Dongdong and TV • Dongdong and TV • Dongdong and TV • Dongdong and TV • Dongdong and TV • Dongdong and TV • Dongdong and TV • Dongdong and TV • Dongdong and TV • Dongdong and TV • Dongdong and TV • Dongdong and TV • Dongdong and TV • Dongdong and TV • Dongdong and TV • Dongdong and TV

看电视

　　今天是星期六。现在是下午两点半，外面很冷，风很大，
又下雨。冬冬的一家人今天都在家里。他们有一部电视机，
可是现在大家都要看电视——冬冬要看第十频道的网球比赛；
弟弟要看第九频道的动画片儿；
妹妹要看第七频道的电视剧；妈
妈要看第一频道的电影；爸爸要
看第二频道的新闻。

Something to know

❀ **Peking opera**

Peking opera, 京剧 jīngjù, originated from local plays and was performed after the harvest in the north of China. It was originally performed on an open stage in the streets or in a temple courtyard, but is now normally performed in a theater. The Peking opera, accompanied by an orchestra, combines singing, dialogue, acting, dancing and acrobatics.

In the play, costumes and facial make-up are used to identify various characters. The four main roles in the play are 生 shēng, 旦 dàn, 净 jìng and 丑 chǒu. Shēng is the leading male role and is normally a scholar, official or a patriot. Dàn is the leading female role and is sometimes played by a male actor. Jìng normally represents a warrior, hero or demon, and chǒu is a civilian or a servant. Chǒu is a comic character and is normally made up with white patches around his eyes and nose. The plots are normally taken from fairy tales, legends, historical stories or literary works. Many older people who go to the theater know the plays by heart and often nod their heads, tap their feet or sing along with their eyes closed. They go to "listen" to the opera, rather than go to "see" the opera.

生 shēng

旦 dàn

净 jìng

丑 chǒu

❀ Chinese orchestra

In southern China, a traditional orchestra can be small with between three and five members. The modern Chinese orchestra may include as many members as a Western orchestra. A great variety of instruments are used, such as 笙 shēng, 箫 xiāo, 笛 dí, 钹 bó, 琵琶 pípá, 二胡 èrhú, 古筝 gǔzhēng and 扬琴 yángqín.

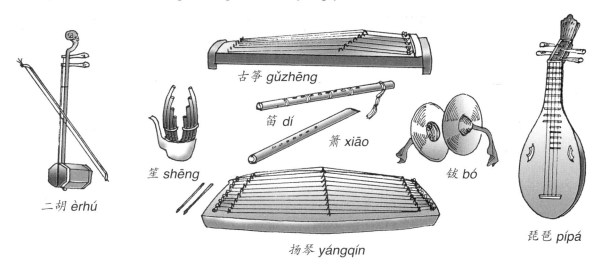

古筝 gǔzhēng

笛 dí

箫 xiāo

笙 shēng

钹 bó

二胡 èrhú

扬琴 yángqín

琵琶 pípá

❀ Dragon dance and lion dance

In Chinese folklore, the dragon can bring rain and the lion can ward off evil spirits. Traditionally, the dragon dance, 舞龙 wǔlóng, is performed at harvest festivals and ceremonies to pray for rain, while the lion dance, 舞狮 wǔshī, is held in the New Year to bring good luck. Nowadays, both dances are seen at all Chinese festivals.

舞龙 wǔlóng

舞狮 wǔshī

dì wǔ kè fù xí
第五课　复习（一）

1 **Letter to a friend**

张英: 你好！

　　我现在住在东山区（qū），上东山中学十一年级九班。东山中学是男女合（hé）校，有三千多个学生。我家离学校很近，只有两公里，所以我天天走路上学。

　　在学校，我最好的朋友是王（wáng）小明、白大伟和李兰兰。王小明很有意思，常常上课迟到，也常常忘了做作业。李兰兰功（gōng）课非（fēi）常好，数学都考九十几分。白大伟汉语说得很流（liú）利，功课也不错。

　　大伟的家离学校不远，他骑（qí）车上学。有时候，他会和我一起走路去学校。大伟很喜欢古典（gǔ diǎn）音乐，还会弹吉他（tán jí）。我现在功（gōng）课不多，我想要他周末教（jiāo）我弹吉他（tán jí）。你最近好吗？请常来信（xìn）。

　　　　祝你

学习好！

　　　　　　　　　　　　　　　　李秋

　　　　　　　　　　　　　　　六月二十九日

2 Letter to a relative

大姨：

　　您好！很久没写信给您了。我爸爸、妈妈都很好。

　　我今年学校功课很多，作业多，考试也多。我晚上常常得开夜车，准备考试。

　　今天学校的汉语老师带我们去中国城。中国城离学校差不多十五公里，坐火车只要十几分钟。我们上午看了一部功夫电影，男生都说很有意思，可是女生都说很无聊。我们中午在一家中国饭馆吃饭。同学们点了古老肉、麻婆豆腐、春卷、炒饭、炒青菜和酸辣汤。大伟说古老肉好吃，小明说酸辣汤不错，可是李秋说古老肉太甜，酸辣汤太酸了。

　　我现在周末在教钢琴，我的学生今年只有五岁，可是她钢琴弹得还不错。

　　祝您

健康！

兰兰

七月十四日

3 A little note

大伟:

因为我昨天晚上看了十一点半的足(zú)球比赛，所以今天早上睡(shuì)过头(tóu)了。你知道吗？今天第一节的英语课，我迟到了；第三节的汉语课，我忘了带(dài)课本；第四节的数学课，我忘了带作业；第六节的科学考试，我忘了准备。

今天晚上第四频(pín)道八点半还有一场比赛，我还要看。明天要交英语作业，我还没做。我今天向(xiàng)兰兰借(jiè)作业，可是兰兰不借我。我看，今天看了球赛以后，我还得开(kāi)夜(yè)车做英语作业。

因为我明天不可以再睡(shuì)过头(tóu)，所以请你明天早上六点打电话给我。我的手(shǒu)机(jī)是新(xīn)的，号码(mǎ)是〇(líng)七一四九五八六三。

请别忘了打电话给我。谢谢！

小明

下午四点半

4 **Language functions**

(1) Asking what subjects someone has

你今天有什么课？　Nǐ jīntiān yǒu shénme kè?

我今天有科学、英语和汉语。　Wǒ jīntiān yǒu kēxué, Yīngyǔ hé Hànyǔ.

他今年有什么课？　Tā jīnnián yǒu shénme kè?

他今年有数学、英语、汉语和历史。　Tā jīnnián yǒu shùxué, Yīngyǔ, Hànyǔ hé lìshǐ.

Asking the subject of a period

你第四节是什么课？　Nǐ dì-sì jié shì shénme kè?

我第四节是音乐。　Wǒ dì-sì jié shì yīnyuè.

她下一节是什么课？　Tā xià yì jié shì shénme kè?

她下一节是美术。　Tā xià yì jié shì měishù.

Asking for a reason

哥哥为什么讨厌上音乐课？　Gēge wèishénme tǎoyàn shàng yīnyuè kè?

因为他没有音乐细胞。　Yīnwèi tā méi yǒu yīnyuè xìbāo.

你为什么不去看电影？　Nǐ wèishénme bú qù kàn diànyǐng?

因为我忘了带钱。　Yīnwèi wǒ wàng le dài qián.

Describing one's talent

我弟弟很有数学头脑。　Wǒ dìdi hěn yǒu shùxué tóunǎo.

我姐姐没有运动细胞。　Wǒ jiějie méi yǒu yùndòng xìbāo.

Asking how someone did in a test

你汉语考得怎么样？　Nǐ Hànyǔ kǎo de zěnmeyàng?

我汉语考得不错。　Wǒ Hànyǔ kǎo de bú cuò.

我汉语考得很差。　Wǒ Hànyǔ kǎo de hěn chà.

Asking the marks of a test

你数学考试得了多少分？　Nǐ shùxué kǎoshì dé le duōshǎo fēn?

我得了八十七分。　Wǒ dé le bāshíqī fēn.

我只得了四十五分。　Wǒ zhǐ dé le sìshíwǔ fēn.

Asking if someone is prepared for an exam

明天的科学考试，你准备了吗？　Míngtiān de kēxué kǎoshì, nǐ zhǔnbèi le ma?

我准备了。　Wǒ zhǔnbèi le.

我还没准备，今天得开夜车了。　Wǒ hái méi zhǔnbèi, jīntiān děi kāi yèchē le.

(2) Stating the grade and class

你在几年级几班？　Nǐ zài jǐ niánjí jǐ bān?

我在十一年级七班。　Wǒ zài shíyī niánjí qī bān.

Asking which school someone attends

你上哪个学校？ Nǐ shàng nǎ gè xuéxiào?

我上大明男子中学。 Wǒ shàng Dàmíng Nánzǐ Zhōngxué.

我上第八中学。 Wǒ shàng Dì-bā Zhōngxué.

Asking the number of students

你们学校有多少学生？ Nǐmen xuéxiào yǒu duōshǎo xuésheng?

我们学校有四千多个学生。 Wǒmen xuéxiào yǒu sì qiān duō gè xuésheng.

我们学校只有四百多个学生。 Wǒmen xuéxiào zhǐ yǒu sì bǎi duō gè xuésheng.

Asking how long someone has learned Chinese

他学习汉语多久了？ Tā xuéxí Hànyǔ duō jiǔ le?

他学习汉语两年多了。 Tā xuéxí Hànyǔ liǎng nián duō le.

Asking the meaning of a word/sentence

"马马虎虎" 是什么意思？ "Mǎmǎ hūhū" shì shénme yìsi?

"马马虎虎" 就是 so so。 "Mǎmǎ hūhū" jiùshì so so.

Seeking permission to borrow something

你的数学作业借我，好吗？ Nǐ de shùxué zuòyè jiè wǒ, hǎo ma?

行，拿去吧！ Xíng, ná qù ba.

不行，作业不借你。 Bù xíng, zuòyè bú jiè nǐ.

Asking if someone has completed something

你英语作业做了吗？ Nǐ Yīngyǔ zuòyè zuò le ma?

做了，我今天上午做了。 Zuò le, wǒ jīntiān shàngwǔ zuò le.

我还没做。 Wǒ hái méi zuò.

作业？我们有数学作业吗？ Zuòyè? Wǒmen yǒu shùxué zuòyè ma?

Asking how to say something in Chinese

"Boring" 的汉语怎么说？ "Boring" de Hànyǔ zěnme shuō?

是 "无聊"。 Shì "wúliáo".

Asking when to hand in an assignment

我们什么时候要交汉语作业？ Wǒmen shénme shíhou yào jiāo Hànyǔ zuòyè?

我们今天要交。 Wǒmen jīntiān yào jiāo.

汉语作业？我们有汉语作业吗？ Hànyǔ zuòyè? Wǒmen yǒu Hànyǔ zuòyè ma?

(3) Asking the mode of transport

你骑自行车上学吗？ Nǐ qí zìxíngchē shàngxué ma?

是的，我骑自行车上学。 Shìde, wǒ qí zìxíngchē shàngxué.

不，我坐公共汽车上学。 Bù, wǒ zuò gōnggòng qìchē shàngxué.

Use of 多 and 几 to state an amount

两个多小时。 Liǎng gè duō xiǎoshí.

三百多块。　Sān bǎi duō kuài.

四十几个小时。　Sìshíjǐ gè xiǎoshí.

五十几分钟。　Wǔshíjǐ fēn zhōng.

Asking the length of time required

你走路到学校要多长时间？　Nǐ zǒulù dào xuéxiào yào duō cháng shíjiān?

要半个多小时。　Yào bàn gè duō xiǎoshí.

Asking where someone lives

你住在哪里？　Nǐ zhù zài nǎli?

我住在中山区。　Wǒ zhùzài Zhōngshān Qū.

我住在悉尼。　Wǒ zhù zài Xīní.

Asking if a place is far away

你家离学校远吗？　Nǐ jiā lí xuéxiào yuǎn ma?

很远，差不多四十公里。　Hěn yuǎn, chàbuduō sìshí gōnglǐ.

我家离学校不远，只有四公里。　Wǒ jiā lí xuéxiào bù yuǎn, zhǐ yǒu sì gōnglǐ.

Giving directions

劳驾，到邮局怎么走？　Láojià, dào yóujú zěnme zǒu?

你往前走，到十字路口往左拐。　Nǐ wǎng qián zǒu, dào shízì lùkǒu wǎng zuǒ guǎi.

你往北走，到十字路口往西拐。　Nǐ wǎng běi zǒu, dào shízì lùkǒu wǎng xī guǎi.

(4) Asking if there is anything good

今天晚上有什么好的电视节目？　Jīntiān wǎnshang yǒu shénme hǎo de diànshì jiémù?

第七频道有一部电视剧，还不错。　Dì-qī píndào yǒu yí bù diànshìjù, hái búcuò.

今天晚上没什么好的节目。　Jīntiān wǎnshang méi shénme hǎo de jiémù.

Use of v + 过 to state past experience

这部电影你看过了吗？　Zhè bù diànyǐng nǐ kàn guò le ma?

看过了，我看过两次了。　Kàn guò le, wo kàn guò liǎng cì le.

我还没看过。我明天去看。　Wǒ hái méi kàn guò. Wǒ míngtiān qù kàn.

Use of 别 + v to give advice

别看电视了，去睡觉！　Bié kàn diànshì le, qù shuìjiào!

别忘了明天要交数学作业。　Bié wàng le míngtiān yào jiāo shùxué zuòyè.

Expressing an interest

你对足球赛有兴趣吗？　Nǐ duì zúqiú sài yǒu xìngqù ma?

有，我是足球迷。　Yǒu, wǒ shì zúqiú mí.

没有，我对足球赛没兴趣。　Méi yǒu, wǒ duì zúqiú sài méi xìngqù.

Use of 迷 to describe a person

哥哥是网球迷，天天看网球赛。　Gēge shì wǎngqiú mí, tiāntiān kàn wǎngqiú sài.

妈妈说我是个电视迷。　Māma shuō wǒ shì gè diànshì mí.

dì liù kè gè yǒu qiān qiū
第六课　各有千秋

1 Do we look alike?

兰兰你好！好久不见。

Wáng shū
王叔叔好！我不是兰兰。我是李秋。

yí   zhǎng
咦？你和兰兰长得真像。

是吗？兰兰比较高，我比较矮。

我的意思是——
yǎn jīng
你们的眼睛很像。

yǎn jīng
眼睛？兰兰的眼睛比较大，

我的眼睛比较小。

那么——是鼻子像。

鼻子？兰兰的鼻子挺，我的塌多了。

奇怪！为什么我觉得你和兰兰长得很像？——我知道了。你们的头发很像。

头发？兰兰的头发短，我的长多了。

我的意思是——你们俩都是黑头发。

2 Am I fat?

你看，她是不是比我瘦？

没错，她比你瘦。

她是不是比我苗条？
(miáo tiáo)

对。她比你苗条，比你瘦。

我想我太胖了。我得减肥。
(jiǎn féi)

你太胖了？你要减肥？

我想，如果我不吃早餐（cān），我就可以跟她一样苗条（miáo tiáo）。

你可以跟她一样苗条？

我看你会跟她一样瘦。

如果你也不吃午餐（cān）和晚餐，你就会比她瘦。

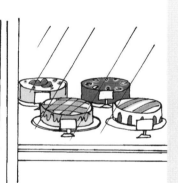

如果我不吃三餐（cān），我吃什么？

我看，你就吃蛋糕（dàn gāo）

和冰淇淋（bīng qí lín）吧！

3 **This is me**

我个子高瘦，有卷头发和小眼睛。我
对音乐没兴趣。我喜欢运动，是球迷。我
的个性很随和。我的朋友说我有幽默
感，可是我爸爸说我做事马马虎虎。

我个子不高，也不瘦。我有短头发和大
眼睛。我的个性比较内向。我喜欢音乐，
可是没有运动细胞。我做事比较认
真，所以我的朋友常说我爱挑剔。

我个子不高，也不胖。我有高鼻子
和大眼睛。我喜欢看足球赛，也喜欢看
科幻电影。我觉得我有科学头脑，
可是我哥哥常说我笨头笨脑的。

我个子瘦小，有长头发、小眼睛和塌鼻子。
我喜欢热门音乐，周末常去听音乐会。我的
个性比较外向，朋友很多。我的朋友常说
我是管家婆。

Learn the sentences

❋ **Use of 比较 in comparison**

When 比较 bǐjiào is followed by an adjective or adverb in comparison, it shows a relative degree of difference, meaning more or less, for example, 比较高, taller; 比较大, bigger.

> 我比较高，我哥哥比较矮。
>
> 她的眼睛(yǎn jīng)比较大，我的比较小。
>
> 这件衣服比较贵，那件比较便宜。
>
> 我数学考得比较好，英语考得比较差。

❋ **Use of 多了 in comparison**

When 多了 is used following an adjective or adverb in comparison, it shows a stronger degree of difference, meaning much more or much less, for example, 高多了, much taller; 大多了, much bigger.

> 我矮，我弟弟高多了。
>
> 她的眼睛小，我的大多了。
>
> 我数学考得好，英语考得差多了。
>
> 这件衣服贵，那件便宜多了。

※ Describing one's appearance using 长得

To describe someone's appearance, 长得 zhǎng de is often used before the description, carrying the meaning of grown to be, i.e. 长得很高 literally means grown very tall.

> 我弟弟长得很高。
>
> 他妹妹长得很漂亮。 piào liàng
>
> 她和她妈妈长得真像。
>
> 我和我姐姐长得不像。

※ Use of 比 in comparison

When 比 is used in comparison as (more) than, it is placed before the subject being compared, for example, 比他高, taller than him.

我比他高。	他比我矮。
她比她姐姐胖。	她姐姐比她瘦。
我比你胖。	你比我瘦。
你的头发比我的长。 tóu fà	我的头发比你的短。
这条裤子比那条贵。 tiáo kù	那条裤子比这条便宜。

【谁高？】

黄蓝比高明高，高明比李伟矮。
陈东比李伟高，比黄蓝矮。 chén

这四个人，谁最高？谁最矮？

✳ **Describing similarity using 跟 x 一样**

When orally describing the similarity between two things, 跟 gēn is often used. It is placed before the subject being compared and followed by 一样, meaning same as, for example, 跟他一样高, as tall as him.

> 我跟爸爸一样高。
>
> 她跟她姐姐一样漂亮。 *piàoliàng*
>
> 我妹妹跟我妈妈一样胖。
>
> 我跟她一样苗条。 *miáo tiáo*
>
> 你的眼睛跟她的一样大。 *yǎn jīng*

我跟爸爸一样高。

 New words and expressions

1

各有千秋	gè yǒu qiānqiū	*idiom.* each has its own merits
好久不见	hǎo jiǔ bú jiàn	*idiom.* long time no see
长	zhǎng	*v.* grow; *adj.* cháng- long
像	xiàng	*adj.* alike; *v.* be like, resemble
比较	bǐjiào	*adv.* comparatively, relatively 比 - to compare; 较 - to compare, relatively
高	gāo	*adj.* tall; high
矮	ǎi	*adj.* short (of stature); low (of houses, tables etc.)

挺	tǐng	*adj.* prominent (nose); *adv.* very
塌	tā	*adj.* flat (nose); *v.* collapse
奇怪	qíguài	*adj.* strange 奇 - strange; 怪 - strange, odd
觉得	juéde	*v.* feel, think 觉 - to feel
俩	liǎ	*colloq.* two (people), also said as 俩儿 liǎr

2

比	bǐ	*prep.* (more) than; *v.* compare
瘦	shòu	*adj.* 1. thin, lean; 2. tight (fitting)
苗条	miáotiáo	*adj.* (of a woman) slim
胖	pàng	*adj.* fat, plump
减肥	jiǎnféi	*v.* lose weight 减 - to reduce, minus; 肥 - fat
如果	rúguǒ	*conj.* if, in case, in the event of 如 - if; 果 - fruit; result
早餐	zǎocān	*n.* breakfast 餐 - meal
跟	gēn	*conj.* and
一样	yíyàng	*adj.* the same, equally, 跟 x 一样 - same as
午餐	wǔcān	*n.* lunch 餐 - meal
晚餐	wǎncān	*n.* dinner 餐 - meal
餐	cān	*n.* meal

3

个子	gèzi	*n.* stature, body build 个 - individual; measure word
卷	juǎn	*adj.* curly; *n.* roll
个性	gèxìng	*n.* personality 个 - individual, m.w.; 性 - nature, character
随和	suíhé	*adj.* amiable, easy to get along with 随 - to follow
幽默感	yōumògǎn	*n.* sense of humor 幽默 - humor; 感 - to sense, feel
做事	zuòshì	*v.* do things
内向	nèixiàng	*adj.* introvert 内 - inside; 向 - towards, to
认真	rènzhēn	*adj.* conscientious, earnest 认 - to recognize; 真 - real, true
爱	ài	*v.* love
挑剔	tiāoti	*v.* nitpick; *adj.* hypercritical 挑 - to choose, to pick; 剔 tī - to pick
笨头笨脑	bèn tóu bèn nǎo	*adj.* stupid, have a thick skull 笨 - stupid; 头 - head; 脑 - brain
外向	wàixiàng	*adj.* extrovert 外 - outside; 向 - towards, to
管家婆	guǎnjiāpó	*n.* a nickname for house keeper 管 - to take charge; 家 - house 婆 - old woman

喜欢谁

对不起！今天不行。今天英英在我家。

她在你家做什么？
我们一块儿看电视。

你喜欢她吗？
fēi
我非常喜欢它。

yǎn jīng
她的眼睛比我的大吗？
对！它的眼睛比你的大。

她比我高吗？
不，它比你矮多了。

bí
她的鼻子比我的鼻子小吗？
不！它的鼻子比你的大多了。

piào liàng
她长得漂亮吗？
它长得一点儿都不漂亮。

那你为什么喜欢她？
ài
因为它很可爱。

……
wèi
喂！你怎么不说话了？

英英是你现在的女朋友吗？
不是。它是我朋友的狗。

！

我的女朋友
yōu mò gǎn
没有幽默感！

Write the characters

见 jiàn *to see*	像 xiàng *alike, to resemble*	较 jiào *to compare, relatively*	高 gāo *tall, high*	矮 ǎi *short (height), low (height)*
觉 jué; jiào *to feel; sleep*	短 duǎn *short (length)*	瘦 shòu *thin, lean; tight (fitting)*	胖 pàng *fat, plump*	如 rú *if*
果 guǒ *fruit; result*	跟 gēn *and*	性 xìng *nature, character*	内 nèi *inside*	向 xiàng *towards, to*

Dongdong's sister • Dongdong's sister • Dongdong's sister • Dongdong's sister • Dongdong's sister

长得很像

冬冬的朋友说，冬冬的妹妹和他妈妈长得很像，可是冬冬的妹妹不觉得她和妈妈长得像。她说，"我妈妈的眼睛比较大，我的比较小；我妈妈比较胖，我比较苗条；我妈妈矮，我高多了；我妈妈的头发短，我的长多了；我妈妈爱挑剔，我有幽默感。我妈妈没音乐细胞，我有音乐细胞；我妈妈没有运动细胞，我有运动细胞。"

Something to know

❋ In all sizes

环肥燕瘦 Huánféi-Yànshòu is a Chinese phrase expressing that attractive women come in all sizes. 环 and 燕 refer to two beauties who were both favorites of Chinese emperors. The former was known to be plump and the latter to be slender.

环 refers to 杨玉环 Yáng Yùhuán, better known as 杨贵妃 Yáng Guìfēi. 杨贵妃 was the beloved concubine of a Tang emperor 玄宗 Xuánzōng in the 8th Century. She was originally with the emperor's son, but the emperor was so enchanted by her beauty that he arranged for her to bcome a Taoist nun to prevent criticism when he later took her for his own. For more than ten years the emperor favored her. Unfortunately during a military rebellion the emperor was forced to order her to hang herself, but his adoration for her continued after her death.

Famous poet 李白 Lǐ Bái from the Tang Dynasty, wrote an epic poem 长恨歌 Chánghèn Gē, *Song of Everlasting Sorrow*, describing the love the emperor had for 杨贵妃 and the sorrow it caused. A section of the poem describes her taking a spring bath, detailing her fair complexion, full figure and delicate qualities. The spring was recreated in 西安 Xī'ān and the site has now become a tourist attraction.

燕 refers to 赵飞燕 Zhào Fēiyàn. She was a much loved concubine of a Han emperor 成帝 Chéngdì in the first Century BC. 飞 means *to fly* and 燕 is *swallow*. 赵飞燕 was a renowned dancer. Her slender figure and graceful movements were akin to that of a flying swallow, which is how her name was derived.

❋ Battle of wits

苏东坡 Sū Dōngpō was a famous writer in the Song Dynasty. His works are still regarded as popular literary classics. There are stories about him battling wits with his sister 苏小妹 Sū Xiǎomèi. 苏小妹 was well educated and literate, which was uncommon for females at that time. It has been said that the two of them were fond of using poetry to rival one another.

Reportedly 苏东坡 had a long face and 苏小妹 had a protruding forehead. On one occasion 苏东坡 wrote a poem teasing his sister, in it he says 未出房门三五步，额头已到画堂前。Wèi chū fángmén sānwǔ bù, étou yǐ dào huàtáng qián. *Out of your room but a few steps ahead, what has reached the hall is your forehead*. In retaliation, 苏小妹 satirized him by replying 去年一滴相思泪，至今流不到腮边。Qùnián yì dī xiāngsī lèi, zhì jīn liú bú dào sāibiān. *Shed last year, but has yet to reach your cheek, is your lovesick tear*.

Although research shows 苏东坡 did not have a younger sister, such stories are well told and often appear in Chinese plays and dramas.

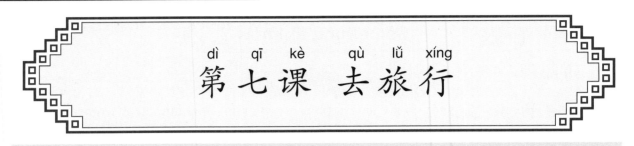

dì qī kè qù lǚ xíng
第七课 去旅行

1 Holiday plans

 大伟，你打算暑假做什么？

我要参加学校的中国旅行。

 小明也参加吗？

 小明也参加。
你不参加吗？

我不打算参加。

 你们要去哪些地方？

我们要去北京和西安。

一共去几天？

一共去九天。

李秋，你参加学校的中国旅行吗？

我不参加。我去过北京和西安了。

那么，你打算暑假做什么？

我要和我妈妈去上海看叔叔。
hǎi　shū

你叔叔住在上海啊？
shū　　hǎi

是啊！我们还要和叔叔一起去桂林玩儿。
guì　lín

你呢？你暑假要去什么地方玩儿？

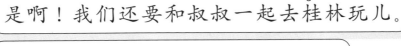

我这个暑假不出去玩儿。
我打算学小提琴。
tí　qín

2 What to bring

From: 王小明

Subject: 带什么东西

To: 李秋

Date: 二〇〇九年九月七日，星期一，10:15 PM

李秋：

　　你们签证办好了吗？因为去中国要办签证，我们

明天得交护照和两张照片。今天下课后我去拍了照片。

兰兰说照片里的我看起来很凶、很胖。我知道兰兰是

开玩笑，因为我觉得照片里的我看起来挺英俊的 :)。

你的行李准备好了吗？不知道现在北京的天气怎么

样，你看我得带什么东西？要不要带相机？

　　小明

From:	李秋
Subject:	Re: 带什么东西
To:	王小明
Date:	二〇〇九年九月八日，星期二，7:24 PM

小明：

　　我们签证已经办好了，机票也买好了，不过我还没准备行李。在中国现在是秋天，天气很凉快。我不打算带太多东西。你也不用带太多东西，带几件 T 恤衫和短裤就可以了。你当然要带相机。北京的秋天很美，你要拍很多照片回来给我们看。还有，别忘了带手机。出去旅行，有了手机就不用担心迷路。

李秋

3 Itinerary

北京、西安的行<ruby>程<rt>chéng</rt></ruby>

九月十九日　坐下午两点半的飞机到东京，在东京过一<ruby>夜<rt>yè</rt></ruby>。

九月二十日　<ruby>从<rt>cóng</rt></ruby>东京坐飞机到北京，在北京过四夜。

　　第一天　从东京坐九点的飞机，十二点到北京机场。

　　第二天　七点吃早饭，八点出<ruby>发<rt>fā</rt></ruby>，参<ruby>观<rt>guān</rt></ruby>长城。

　　第三天　六点半吃早饭，七点半出发，参观<ruby>紫<rt>zǐ</rt></ruby><ruby>禁<rt>jìn</rt></ruby>城和天<ruby>坛<rt>tán</rt></ruby>。

　　第四天　六点半吃早饭，七点半出发，参观<ruby>颐<rt>yí</rt></ruby>和<ruby>园<rt>yuán</rt></ruby>和明<ruby>陵<rt>líng</rt></ruby>。

九月二十四日 坐火车去西安，在西安过两<ruby>夜<rt>yè</rt></ruby>。

　　第一天　从北京坐六点的火车，下午两点到西安。

　　第二天　七点吃早饭，八点出发，参观<ruby>秦<rt>qín</rt></ruby><ruby>始<rt>shǐ</rt></ruby><ruby>皇<rt>huáng</rt></ruby>的<ruby>兵<rt>bīng</rt></ruby><ruby>马<rt>yǒng</rt></ruby>俑和大<ruby>雁<rt>yàn</rt></ruby><ruby>塔<rt>tǎ</rt></ruby>。

九月二十六日 从西安坐飞机到东京，在东京过一夜。

九月二十七日 下午四点五十分

　　　　　　　回到机场。

Learn the sentences

❋ **Asking about a plan**

To ask What do you plan to do? say 你打算做什么？The 打算 comes from do calculation on the abacus, 算盘 suànpán, which is essential when making a plan. To answer, state the plan.

你打算暑假做什么？	我打算暑假去旅行。
你打算周末做什么？	我要去听(tīng)音乐(yuè)会。
哥哥打算明年去什么地方玩儿？	他打算去北京玩儿。

❋ **Use of 些 as a measure word**

When 些 is used as a measure word, it indicates a plural number, i.e. 哪些地方 means which places. For comparison, 哪个地方 means which place and 什么地方 means what (is the) place.

你们要去哪些地方？	我们要去上海(hǎi)和北京。
他们要去哪些地方？	他们要去香港(xiāng gǎng)、台(tái)北和北京。
你要去旅行？去哪些地方？	我要去悉尼(xī ní)、墨尔本(mò ěr)和堪培拉(kān péi lā)。
他要去旅行？去哪些地方？	他要去旧金山(jiù jīn)、纽约(niǔ yuē)和伦敦(lún dūn)。

❋ **More uses of v + 过 for past experiences**

v + 过 is used to express a past experience. In lesson four, we have learned 看过, have seen. Here are more examples of using different verbs: 去过, have been to; 吃过, have eaten.

你们看过这部电影吗？	看过，我们看过两次(cì)了。
你爸爸去过北京吗？	他去过北京了。
你吃过龙眼(lóng yǎn)吗？	我没吃过龙眼。

✳ **Use of v + 好了 for emphasizing**

When 好了 is used after a verb, it emphasizes the task being fully completed, for example,
办好了, fully arranged; 买好了, already bought; 做好了, completely done.

你签证办好了吗？ _{qiān zhèng bàn}	我签证已经办好了。
你们机票买好了吗？	我们机票还没买。
弟弟功课做好了吗？ _{gōng}	他说他已经做好了。
明天的考试，你准备好了吗？	还没。我今天晚上得开夜车。 _{kāi yè}

✳ **Use of 从……到**

To state from ... to, use 从……到, for example, 从东京坐飞机到北京, take the airplane
from Tokyo to Beijing.

爸爸昨天从北京坐飞机到东京。 _{cóng}
哥哥明天要从北京坐火车到南京。
弟弟今天上午从家里走路到火车站。

 New words and expressions

1			
旅行	lǚxíng	*n. v.* travel 旅 - to travel; 行 - to go; OK
打算	dǎsuàn	*v.* intend, plan; *n.* intention, plan 算 - to calculate
暑假	shǔjià	*n.* summer vacation 暑 - heat, hot weather; 假 - holiday
参加	cānjiā	*v.* attend, take part in 参 - to participate; 加 - to add
些	xiē	*m.w.* a few, a little
地方	dìfāng	*n.* place 地 - land, ground; 方 - direction
西安	Xī'ān	the capital city of Shaanxi (陕西 Shǎnxī) province where the entombed terracotta warriors were excavated 西 - west; 安 - peace, peaceful
上海	Shànghǎi	*n.* Shanghai, the largest city in China 海 - sea

一起	yìqǐ	*adv.* together　起 - to get up, to rise	
桂林	Guìlín	*n.* a city in Guangxi, which is famous for its spectacular limestone scenery　桂 - laurel; 林 - forest	
玩儿	wánr	*v.* play, have fun　玩 - to play, to have fun	

2

签证	qiānzhèng	*n.* visa　签 - to sign; 证 - to prove, certificate
办	bàn	*v.* handle, manage
护照	hùzhào	*n.* passport　护 - to protect; 照 - to take (photos); photo
照片	zhàopiàn	*n.* photograph　照 - to take (photos); 片 - thin piece
拍	pāi	*v.* take (photographs); hit (with palm of hand)
开玩笑	kāi wánxiào	*v.* joke, make fun of　开 - to open; 玩 - to play; 笑 - to laugh
英俊	yīngjùn	*adj.* handsome
行李	xíngli	*n.* luggage, baggage　行 - to go; 李 lǐ - plum, Lǐ - a surname
相机	xiàngjī	*n.* camera　相 - appearance; 机 - machine
已经	yǐjīng	*adv.* already　已 - already; 经 - to pass through
机票	jīpiào	*n.* airline ticket　（飞）机 - airplane ; 票 - ticket
不过	búguò	*conj.* however, but
不用	búyòng	*adv.* need not
短裤	duǎnkù	*n.* shorts　短 - short; 裤 - pants, trousers
当然	dāngrán	*adj.* of course, without doubt
美	měi	*adj.* beautiful
担心	dānxīn	*v.* worry　担 - to shoulder; 心 - heart
迷路	mílù	*v.* lose one's way　迷 - to be lost, enthusiast; 路 - road

3

行程	xíngchéng	*n.* itinerary　行 - to go; OK; 程 - journey, distance
飞机	fēijī	*n.* airplane　飞 - to fly; 机 - machine
东京	Dōngjīng	*n.* Tokyo　东 - east; 京 - capital
过夜	guòyè	*v.* spend the night, stay overnight　夜 - night
从	cóng	*prep.* from
机场	jīchǎng	*n.* airport　（飞）机 - airplane; 场 - field
出发	chūfā	*v.* set out, start off　出 - to go out; 发 - fā, to emit; fà, hair

☺

参观	cānguān	*v.* visit
长城	Chángchéng	*n.* the Great Wall　长 - long; 城 - city wall, city
紫禁城	Zǐjìnchéng	*n.* the Forbidden City
天坛	Tiāntán	*n.* Temple of Heaven

颐和园	Yíhé Yuán	n. Summer Palace
明陵	Míng Líng	n. Ming Tombs
秦始皇	Qín Shǐhuáng	n. Qin Emperor　始 - to start; 皇 - emperor
兵马俑	Bīngmǎyǒng	n. Terracotta Warriors　兵 - soldier; 马 - horse
大雁塔	Dà Yàn Tǎ	n. Great Wild Goose Pagoda
香港	Xiānggǎng	n. Hong Kong　香 - fragrant; 港 - port
台北	Táiběi	n. Taipei
墨尔本	Mò'ěrběn	n. Melbourne
堪培拉	Kānpéilā	n. Canberra
旧金山	Jiùjīnshān	n. San Francisco　旧 - old; 金 - gold; 山 - mountain

帮我带去

我想假期去旅行。

你打算去什么地方？

我想去上海。

不要去上海。
上海我去过了，
人太多了。

你看西安怎么样？

别去西安。西安我
去过了，很无聊。

去伦敦吧！我姐姐住
在伦敦，她可以带你
去玩。

好！我买去伦敦
的机票。

这是你的机票。

来！这是我姐姐的。
请你带去给她。

Write the characters

旅 lǚ to travel	算 suàn to calculate	暑 shǔ heat, hot weather	假 jià holiday; leave of absence	参 cān to participate
加 jiā to add	些 xiē [m.w.] a few, some	地 dì land, ground	方 fāng direction	安 ān peace, peaceful
玩 wán to play, to have fun	照 zhào to take (photos); photo	片 piàn; piān thin piece or slice; film	带 dài to take, to bring	相 xiàng appearance, photo
机 jī machine	已 yǐ already	经 jīng to pass through	手 shǒu hand	飞 fēi to fly

Dongdong's trip · Dongdong's trip · Dongdong's trip · Dongdong's trip · Dongdong's trip · Dongdong's trip · Dongdong's trip · Dongdong's trip · Dongdong's trip · Dongdong's trip · Dongdong's trip · Dongdong's trip · Dongdong's trip · Dongdong's trip · Dongdong's trip · Dongdong's trip

去日本

冬冬这个暑假要和爸爸去日本旅行，一共去十七天。今天上午冬冬的爸爸要冬冬去办签证(bàn)。办签证(qiān zhèng)的地方离他们家不远，差不多三公里，走路只要半个小时。冬冬走路到那儿，可是忘了带照片。他就回家拿(ná)照片，再走路去。到了那儿，冬冬说："糟糕(zāo gāo)！我忘了带护照(hù)。"

Something to know

🏵 The Great Wall of China

长城 Chángchéng, the Great Wall of China, was first built by 秦始皇 Qín Shǐhuáng, the First Emperor, at around 221 BC. During the Warring States Period, most states built their own territory walls to defend themselves. After Qin Shihuang defeated all states and united the country, he joined the walls along the northern border into one great wall to fence off the aggressive northern invaders. The wall was rebuilt several times and often at different locations. It has been estimated that around two to three million people died from building the wall in its long history.

The Great Wall we see today was mostly rebuilt in the Ming Dynasty in the 15th Century and stretches around 7,000km. It was strategically built in places that were difficult to reach, particularly on top of the mountain ranges. The material and size of the wall varied locally, with an average height of 7-8m, an average width of 6-7m at the base and 4-5m at the top. Gates, watchtowers and beacon towers ran along the wall and it was guarded by around 1,000,000 soldiers.

Most of the wall has now become ruins, although traces can still be seen from outer space. Some sections were renovated in the 20th Century for tourist purposes, with the most popular destinations being the gate 居庸关 Jūyōng Guān and the section at 八达岭 Bādálǐng near Beijing.

🏵 The Forbidden City

紫禁城 Zǐjìnchéng, the Forbidden City, was the Imperial Palace of the Ming and Qing Dynasties. It was first built in 1406 and took 14 years to complete. The palace covered an area of 720,000m² and was surrounded by 10m high walls and a 52m wide river. For over 500 years, 24 emperors lived and ruled China from this palace. It is now called 故宫博物院 Gùgōng Bówùyuàn, Palace Museum, and houses many historical Chinese treasures.

🏵 The Summer Palace

颐和园 Yíhé Yuán, Summer Palace, is an imperial garden of the Qing Dynasty. The palace buildings sit on a mountain facing south towards a large lake, with a 728m long artistic corridor at the foot of the mountain. Empress Cixi Dawger and Emperor Guangxu spent a substantial amount of time in this palace.

The Temple of Heaven

天坛 Tiāntán, Temple of Heaven, is a complex that the Ming and Qing emperors visited every year to worship and pray for a good year of harvest. Its circular praying hall 祈年殿 Qínián Diàn is the most symbolic building.

Ming Tombs

Ming tombs, 明陵 Míng Líng, is a complex where thirteen of the Ming emperors were buried. Each emperor had his own above-ground mausoleum and underground tomb. Not all tombs are open to the public. The two most visited are the mausoleum of Chang Ling and the excavated underground tomb of Ding Ling. The 神道 Shéndào, Spiritual Path, lined with stone statues and stretching 7km, connects the thirteen mausoleums and is a spectacular walk way for tourists.

Terracotta Warriors

Xi'an was the capital city of many dynasties. The first emperor 秦始皇 Qin Shǐhuáng ruled his country and died there. According to historical records, his underground mausoleum is a complex palace filled with treasures. His tomb lies beneath a 51m high hill surrounded by some 400 burial pits. In 1974, local farmers accidentally dug up some terracotta warriors leading to the discovery of three pits of terracotta figures consisting of military array and an official parade. It is estimated there are around 7,000 terracotta figures, chariots, horses and weapons, but the majority of it is still underground. A small section of the uncovered area is now open to tourists, known as the Terracotta Warriors, 兵马俑 Bīngmǎyǒng. As to the tomb itself, it is still untouched and remains a mystery.

Great Wild Goose Pagoda

大雁塔 Dà Yàn Tǎ, Great Wild Goose Pagoda, was built in 652 AD in the Tang Dynasty in Xi'an. It housed the Chinese Buddhist scriptures translated by 玄奘 Xuán Zàng, the monk who travelled to India to collect the Buddhist scripts. The pagoda now stands at 64m tall and takes in the entire view of the city of Xi'an.

1 I am not feeling well

2 Taking sick leave

二〇〇九年十月七日　　星期三　　天气阴雨

我病了，肚子疼，又拉肚子，也发烧，体温三十八度七。早上爸爸打电话到学校，帮我请了一天病假，让我去看医生。上午九点半，妈妈带我去看医生。医生说我是吃坏了肚子，还给了我药。他说，"一天三次，一次两粒，饭后吃"。我昨天也没吃什么东西，不知道为什么会吃坏肚子，真是倒霉。

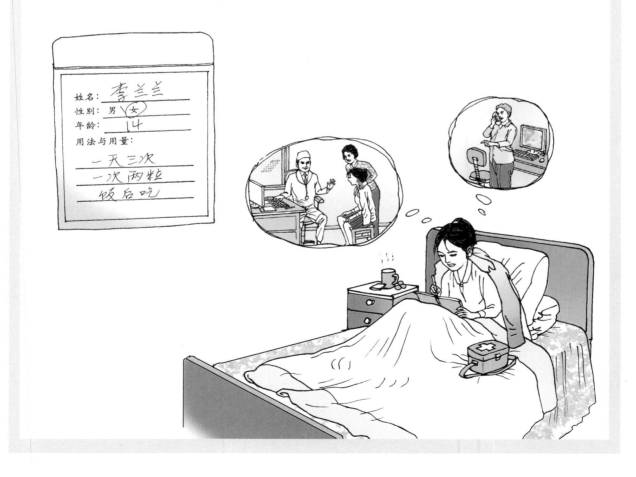

二〇〇九年十月八日　　星期四　　天气晴

我感冒了，发烧，打喷嚏（pēn tì），喉咙（hóu lóng）疼，也咳嗽（ké sòu）。

昨天早上爸爸打电话到学校，帮（bāng）我请了两天病假，让（ràng）我在家休息（xiū xī）。妈妈说小感冒不用看医生，也不用（yòng）吃药。她要我多吃水果，多喝水，多休息（xiū xī）。

我今天不发烧了，可是喉咙（hóu lóng）还疼，也还咳嗽（ké sòu）。最近很多人感冒。我平常很少感冒，不知道为什么这次会感冒，真是倒霉（dǎo méi）。

3 I am feeling better

兰兰，你怎么前天没来上课？

我吃坏了肚子；肚子疼，又拉肚子。

是吃了什么东西？

我不知道，真是倒霉。

去看医生了吗？

去看医生了，也吃药了。

现在好点儿了吗？

现在没事了，谢谢。

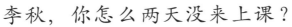

李秋，你怎么两天没来上课？

我感冒了，发烧、头疼、
喉咙疼（hóu lóng）、打喷嚏（pēn tì），也咳嗽（ké sòu）。

最近很多人感冒。你去看医生了吗？

没去，就是在家休息了两天（xiū xī）。

现在好点儿了吗？

现在好多了，只是还咳嗽（ké sòu）。

Learn the sentences

✻ **Asking what happened using 怎么**

We have learned to use 怎么 before a verb to mean why or how, e.g.

你怎么没做作业？　Why didn't you do your homework?

到火车站怎么走？　How do I get to the train station?

怎么 can also be used without a verb but followed by 了 to inquire about what has happened, i.e. 你怎么了？　means What happened to you? or What's wrong with you? To answer, state the situation.

你怎么了？	我感冒了。
弟弟怎么了？	他发烧了。
我们的数学老师怎么了？	他病了，今天不来上课。
姐姐怎么了？	她吃坏了肚子。

✻ **Inquiring about someone's illness**

When someone is not feeling well, 哪里 is used to clarify which area is troubling the person, i.e. 你哪里不舒服？　literally means Where do you feel sick? It is a common question asked by the doctor or parents. To answer, state the situation.

你哪里不舒服？	我头疼，喉咙^{hóu lóng}也疼。
怎么样？你哪里不舒服？	我发烧、打喷嚏^{pēn tì}，也咳嗽^{ké sòu}。
妹妹哪里不舒服？	她肚子疼。

【你知道吗？】

他病了，可是不去看病；病好了，再去看病。

为什么？你知道吗？

❋ Stating a probability

可能, maybe or probably, is usually used before the verb or a stative verb. To state I have probably caught a cold say 我可能感冒了。

> 我可能感冒了。
>
> 弟弟可能发烧了。
>
> 今天下午可能会下雨。
>
> 数学老师今天可能不来上课。

❋ "没 + v" vs "不 + v"

To express something did not happen in the past, use 没 + v, for example, 他没去。He did not go. While 不 + v can also be used for something that did not happen, it signifies this was due to an unwillingness, for example, 他不去。He did not want to go

did not	did not want to
上个星期六他没去看电影。	上个星期六他不去看电影。
昨天姐姐没去看医生。	昨天姐姐不去看医生。
今天妹妹没吃早饭。	今天妹妹不吃早饭。

However, 没 + v cannot be used for something that will not happen in the future, 不 + v is used regardless of the reason.

> 他下个星期六不去看电影。
>
> 姐姐明天不去看医生。
>
> 妹妹明天不吃早饭。

✳ **Use of 次 to state frequency**

To state frequency, 次 is used, e.g. 一天一次, once a day; 一天两次, twice a day; 两天一次, once every two days.

> 一天一次，一次两粒。
>
> 一天三次，一次三粒。
>
> 两个月一次，一次十个人。
>
> 一个星期三次，一次两个小时。

✳ **Asking if someone is feeling better**

To ask Are you feeling better? say 你好点儿了吗？ The answer varies according to the situation. For fully OK, say 没事了; for a lot better, say 好多了; for a little better, say 好点儿了; for not better, say 没有.

你现在好点儿了吗？	我现在没事了，谢谢你。
他今天好点儿了吗？	他今天好多了。
你感冒好点儿了吗？	好点儿了。
你弟弟好点儿了吗？	没有，他还发烧。

New words and expressions

1

病	bìng	*adj.* sick; *n.* illness
疼	téng	*v.* ache, also said as 痛 tòng
		头疼 - (have a) headache; 肚子疼 - (have a) stomachache
喉咙	hóulóng	*n.* throat, also said as 嗓子 sǎngzi
发烧	fāshāo	*v.* have a temperature, run a fever
		发 - to emit (fà- hair); 烧 - to burn
可能	kěnéng	*adv.* maybe, probably 可 - may; 能 - to be able to
感冒	gǎnmào	*v.* have a cold; *n.* cold, flu 感 - to feel; 冒 - to emit, to risk
点儿	diǎnr	*adv.* a little, short for 一点儿
回家	huíjiā	*v.* go home 回 - to return; 家 - home
休息	xiūxi	*v.* rest, take a rest 休 - to rest; 息 xī - breath
先	xiān	*adv.* first, in advance
没事	méishì	*adj.* alright, e.g. 你没事吧？ Are you alright?
		v. have no business, e.g. 我今天没事。 I am free today.
肚子	dùzi	*n.* tummy, abdomen
拉肚子	lā dùzi	*v.* have diarrhoea 拉 - to pull; to play (violin); 肚子 - tummy

---

2

体温	tǐwēn	*n.* body temperature 体 - body; 温 - warm, warmth
帮	bāng	*v.* help, assist
请	qǐng	*v.* 1. ask, e.g. 请假 qǐngjià - ask for leave; 2. please; 3. invite
病假	bìngjià	*n.* sick leave 病 - sick; 假 - leave of absence; holiday
让	ràng	*v.* let, allow
吃坏了肚子	chī huài le dùzi	*colloq.* ate something bad that upset the stomach
		坏 - *adj.* bad; *v.* to go bad
药	yào	*n.* medicine
粒	lì	*m.w.* [for small objects, e.g. tablets, buttons etc.]
倒霉	dǎoméi	*v.* have bad luck 倒 - upside down; 霉 - mould
打喷嚏	dǎ pēntì	*v.* sneeze 打 - to make, to hit, to play, to dial; 喷嚏 - sneeze
咳嗽	késòu	*v.* cough
水	shuǐ	*n.* water
最近	zuìjìn	*n.* recently, lately 最 - most; 近 - near
少	shǎo	*adv.* seldom; *adj.* few, little

发烧了

起床！要上学了！

可是我发烧了，你看！

qǐ chuáng

wa　　　　dù
哇！四十二度七！
你是发烧了！

你头疼吗？　我头疼。

hóu lóng
喉咙疼吗？　喉咙也疼。

肚子疼吗？　肚子也疼。

ké sòu
你咳嗽吗？
咳！咳！我也咳嗽。

你是不是感冒了？
我是感冒了。

所以今天不上学了？
不上学，今天要请病假。

我看，等一会儿我带你去看医生。
不！不要看医生。

那么，喝中药吧！
我不要喝中药！

看看是不是还发烧。
现在不发烧了。我的感冒好了，我去上学。

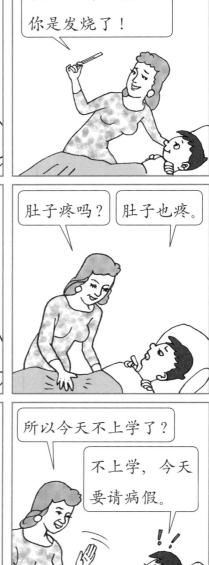

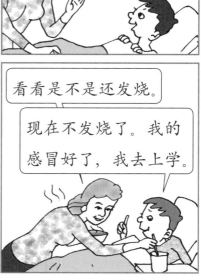

Write the characters

病 bìng *sick, illness*	舒 shū *comfortable*	头 tóu *head*	疼 téng *to ache*	发 fā; fà *to emit; hair*
烧 shāo *to burn*	能 néng *to be able to*	感 gǎn *to feel, sense*	冒 mào *to emit, to risk*	肚 dù *abdomen*
医 yī *doctor, medicine*	坏 huài *bad; to go bad*	药 yào *medicine*	次 cì *time (frequency)*	水 shuǐ *water*

Dongdong's sick day · Dongdong's sick day · Dongdong's sick day · Dongdong's sick day · Dongdong's sick day · Dongdong's sick day

生 病

冬冬吃坏了肚子。他今天早上肚子疼，
拉(lā)肚子。他妈妈帮(bāng)他请了一天病假。冬冬
的朋友黄明南今天感冒了。他又(yòu)打喷嚏(pēn tì)又咳(ké)
嗽(sòu)，他爸爸也帮(bāng)他
请了一天病假，让(ràng)他在家休息(xiū xi)。中午
十二点，黄明南打电话给冬冬。他说今
天有一部电影很好看。下午两点半，他
们俩(liǎ)就一起(qǐ)去看电影。

Something to know

❀ Medical Care

In China, medical care for workers is generally provided by the government. Each work unit, 单位 dānwèi, has its own clinic with general practitioners and provides medicine free of charge. Hospitals are run by the government and the fees are low. This, however, is changing due to the introduction of privatization. In Taiwan, clinics are run privately and there are both private and public hospitals. Medical charges are generally high, however, public servants have their own medical insurance fund, and medical insurance funds for the general public are increasing in popularity.

While Western medicine has been used in general clinics and hospitals, traditional Chinese medicine still plays a role in the medical care of the Chinese people. In some hospitals, traditional Chinese medicine is combined with Western medicine.

❀ Chinese medicine

The Chinese believe that illness is caused by an imbalance of 阴 yīn and 阳 yáng in the body and, therefore, the best cure is to use a natural medicine to help patients adjust this imbalance. Chinese medicine, 中药 zhōngyào, is obtained from nature. Almost 90% of the medicine comes from plants with the remainder from minerals and animals. A Chinese doctor makes a diagnosis by feeling the pulse of his patient. He places his three middle fingers on the patient's wrist to feel their pulse. His diagnosis is made according to the depth, speed, strength and rhythm of the patient's pulse, aided by his observations and the patient's complaints. He then prescribes a combination of herbs for treatment.

The herbs are covered with water in a pot and boiled until the liquid has reduced to the volume of a rice bowl. The herbal tea is then drunk, usually before bedtime. The same batch of herbs is reboiled the next morning and drunk before breakfast. One prescription usually contains three batches of herbs for three days treatment. This is followed by a second appointment. The doctor then feels the change in the patient's pulse to determine the effect of the herbs.

(Top) The Chinese herb 人参 rénshēn
(Right) A Chinese doctor feels the pulse of his patient

He then modifies the prescription by changing some herbs, or changing the quantity of herbs according to the patient's condition. Because of modern technology, Chinese herbs can now be extracted and made into powder or pills for direct consumption.

Chinese herbs are not only used to cure illness, but some are used to strengthen the body. In winter, herbs with yáng property, such as 当归 dāngguī, lingusticum, and 人参 rénshēn, ginseng, are used by most people to help fight winter chills. Steamed chicken or duck soup with herbs is most enjoyable. Some Western doctors believe that Chinese medicine, although taking longer to become effective, is more friendly to the human body and has fewer side effects than antibiotics. The use of some animal products such as deer antlers, rhinoceros horns and tiger bones, however, are a cause of concern for the National Environmental Conservation Group.

❀ Acupuncture

Acupuncture and moxibustion, 针灸 zhēnjiǔ, are common therapies among the Chinese. Acupuncture uses long needles and moxibustion uses heat on certain points of the body to stimulate the flow of 气 qì, energy. Acupuncture is based on the theory that qì flows freely and actively in a healthy body. When the body is unwell, the flow of qì is upset and needs to be stimulated. It is believed by Western doctors that these points relate to nerve trunks and junctions. The insertion of needles into these points can also help produce substances to block pain or to increase the body's immune system. Acupuncture anaesthesia has been successfully used in surgical operations. The practice of acupuncture has also become popular in the West.

The 12 major channels as used in acupuncture

任脉
front midline channel

手太阴肺经
lung channel of hand-taiyin

手厥阴心包经
pericardium channel of hand-jueyin

手少阴心经
heart channel of hand-shaoyin

足厥阴肝经
liver channel of foot-jueyin

足太阴脾经
spleen channel of foot-taiyin

足少阴肾经
kidney channel of foot-shaoyin

足阳明胃经
stomach channel of foot-yangming

督脉
back midline channel

手太阳小肠经
small intestine channel of hand-taiyang

手少阳三焦经
sanjiao channel of hand-shaoyang

手阳明大肠经
large intestine channel of hand-yangming

足太阳膀胱经
urinary bladder channel of foot-taiyang

足少阳胆经
gall bladder channel of foot-shaoyang

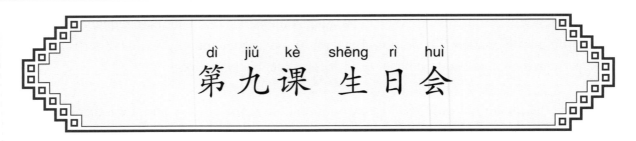

dì jiǔ kè shēng rì huì
第九课　生日会

1 **An invitation**

　　小明的生日快到了，他想在家里开一个生日会。
　　　　　　　　　　　　　　　　yāo kǎ
这是他寄给朋友的邀请卡——

朋友们：
　　　　　　　　　　　　　　　　　　　　qìng
　　八月十六日是我的生日，到我家一起庆祝
吧！时间是下午六点半到晚上十一点。

　　　　　　　　　　　　　　　　　　小明

　　　　　　　　　　　　　　　二〇〇九年八月七日

　　　　　　　　　　　　　　　　　　　　　　　　kǎ
　　今天小明收到了一个中国朋友寄给他的生日卡——

小明：

　　祝你生日快乐！

　　　　　　黄中南

下面是李秋、兰兰和大伟发给小明的短信：

小明：

谢谢你的邀(yāo)请。我八月十六日一定(dìng)准时参加。

李秋

发信时间：八月七日十九时五分

小明：

谢谢你的邀(yāo)请。很对不起，我八月十六日
有事不能参加。你们好好玩儿吧！

兰兰

发信时间：八月八日八时三十分

小明：

你的生日会我当然(dāng rán)参加。你要什么生日礼物？

大伟

发信时间：八月十一日三时十八分

2 The best birthday present

3 Dawei's diary

大伟的日记_{jì}

二〇〇九年八月十六日　天气　晴／阴

今天是小明的生日，他在家里开了一个生日会。小明家今天很热闹_{nào}，吃的东西很多。他妈妈还做了寿面给我们吃。

小明的妈妈说，中国人过生日，以前都吃寿面。吃寿面的意思是因为面很长，所以吃了可以长寿。不过，现在很多人过生日都吃生日蛋糕，不吃寿面了。

小明的妈妈在中国住过两年。她很会做中国菜，还会做中国过节的食品_{shí pǐn}。中国人端午节吃粽子，中秋节吃月饼，春节吃年糕和饺子。我吃过月饼和饺子，可是没吃过年糕和粽子。

 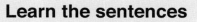

Learn the sentences

✳ **Asking what present to give**

To ask What present are you going to give him? say 你要送他什么礼物？ To answer, replace 什么礼物 with the type of present.

你要送他什么礼物？	我要送他一本书。
你要送我什么生日礼物？	我要送你一条裤子。
你哥哥送你什么生日礼物？	他送我一个手机。

tiáo kù appears above 条裤 in 我要送你一条裤子。

✳ **More use of 又**

We have learned to use 又 repeatedly to describe parallel conditions of something, e.g.

这件又好看又便宜。 This one looks good and is cheap.
这件又不好看又贵。 This one doesn't look good and is expensive.

又 can also be used to describe unfavorable conditions of two different things. In this case 又 is only placed in the second statement, e.g.

这件不好看，那件又太贵。 This one doesn't look good, and that one is too expensive.

这件不好看；那件又太贵。
便宜的我不喜欢；我喜欢的又太贵。
tiáo qún *féi* 这条裙子太肥；那条又太瘦。

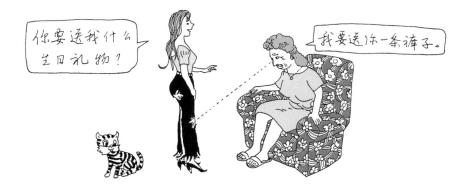

✳ Use of v + 到

When 到 is used as a verb, it means arrive or go to. 到 can also be used after a verb as a supplement to indicate an achievement of the action, for example, 收到, received; 买到, successfully bought.

> 我今天收到爸爸给我的信。
>
> 哥哥今天没收到女朋友的信。
>
> 妈妈今天买到了很好吃的蛋糕。
>
> 姐姐今天没买到她喜欢的衣服。

✳ Use of 看上

When you 看上 something (or someone), it means you take a liking to it because it is up to your standard. If it is not up to your standard and you don't like it, use 看不上.

> tiáo lián　qún
> 姐姐看上了那条连衣裙。
>
> 他看上了我姐姐。
>
> 妈妈看不上哥哥的女朋友。
>
> 哥哥看不上我送的礼物。

New words and expressions

1	生日会	shēngrì huì	n. birthday party
	开	kāi	v. hold (a meeting, exhibition etc.), e.g. 开生日会 kāi shēngrì huì- have a birthday party, 开音乐会 kāi yīnyuè huì- have a concert; open
	寄	jì	v. send, post, mail
	邀请	yāoqǐng	v. invite
	卡	kǎ	n. card, short for 卡片 kǎpiàn
	庆祝	qìngzhù	v. celebrate
	收	shōu	v. receive, collect

到	dào	1. *suppl.* [used after a verb to indicate an achievement], e.g. 收到 - received; 看到 - saw 2. *v.* go to, arrive; 3. *prep.* to
发	fā	*v.* send out, emit; *n.* fà- hair
信	xìn	*n.* letter
短信	duǎnxìn	*n.* text message 短 - short; 信 - letter (mail)
一定	yídìng	*adv.* certainly
准时	zhǔnshí	*adj.* on time, punctual 准 - standard; 时 - time
礼物	lǐwù	*n.* present, gift 礼 - courtesy, ritual; 物 - object, thing

2

送	sòng	*v.* give something as a present
真是的	zhēnshìde	*colloq.* a remark on something unpleasant
说曹操，曹操就到 shuō Cáo Cāo, Cáo Cāo jiù dào		speak of the devil. 曹操 (155-220 A.D.) was the ruler of Wei during the Age of the Three Kingdoms. He was known as being very capable but crafty and evil.
啰唆	luōsuō	*adj.* long-winded
看上	kànshàng	*v.* fancy, take a liking to

3

日记	rìjì	*n.* diary 日 - day; sun; 记 - to record
热闹	rènào	*adj.* lively, bustling with noise and excitement
寿面	shòumiàn	*n.* birthday noodles 寿 - longevity; 面 - noodles
面	miàn	*n.* noodles; mian - side (as in 里面)
长寿	chángshòu	*n.* long life, longevity
过节	guòjié	*v.* celebrate festivals 过 - to pass; 节 - festival; section
食品	shípǐn	*n.* food
端午节	Duānwǔjié	*n.* Dragon Boat Festival 端 - up right; 午 - noon (the fifth day of the fifth lunar month)
粽子	zòngzi	*n.* dumplings made of sticky rice, wrapped in bamboo or reed leaves
中秋节	Zhōngqiūjié	*n.* Mid-Autumn Festival, also called Moon Festival (the 15th day of the eighth lunar month)
月饼	yuèbǐng	*n.* moon cake 月 - moon; 饼 - biscuit, cake
春节	Chūnjié	*n.* Spring Festival, also called 新年 xīnnián in Taiwan (the beginning days of the lunar year)
年糕	niángāo	*n.* New Year's cake, made of sticky rice flour 糕 - cake
饺子	jiǎozi	*n.* dumpling, in the shape of a gold ingot

不吃

喂！

wèi

美英，你明天有空吗？

有什么事吗？

！

我想请你到我家吃饭，庆祝我的生日。

qìng

你的生日是什么时候？

我的生日 shi wu 号，明天。

shi wu 号是下个星期天，不是明天。

没错啊！明天 shi wu 号。

明天 shi wu 号？不对！啊！明天 shi... wu 号。

好啊！我明天什么时候去？

你明天下午来，我请你晚上 chi shuijiao。

你说什么？晚上 qu shuijiao？

对啊！我喜欢 chi shuijiao。你也会喜欢 chi shuijiao。

你喜欢 qu shuijiao，你自己 qu shuijiao。我不去。

shuijiao 好 chi，不知道为什么她不 chi。

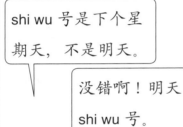

Write the characters

开	寄	起	收	信
kāi *to hold; to open; to start*	jì *to send, to post, to mail*	qǐ *to rise, to get up*	shōu *to receive, to collect*	xìn *letter (mail)*
礼	送	又	寿	蛋
lǐ *courtesy, ritual*	sòng *to give sth. as a present*	yòu *and, again*	shòu *longevity*	dàn *egg*
糕	端	粽	饼	饺
gāo *cake, pudding*	duān *up right*	zòng *dumpling (in bamboo leaves)*	bǐng *biscuit, cake*	jiǎo *dumpling (gold ingot-shaped)*

ent · Dongdong's present · Dongdong's present · Dongdong's present · Dongdong's

present · Dongdong's present · Dongdong's

Dongdong's present · Dongdong's present · Dongdong's present · Dongdong's present · Dongdong's present · Dongdong's present · Do

生 日

　　明天是冬冬妹妹的生日。今天冬冬去百货商店 (huò shāng diàn) 买生日礼物给他妹妹。冬冬看了很多东西，可是不知道要买什么。冬冬想："妹妹喜欢热门 (mén) 音乐；我喜欢古典 (gǔ diǎn) 音乐。我今年的生日，妹妹买了热门音乐给我。我想，妹妹的生日，我就买古典音乐给她吧！"

Something to know

❀ Addressing envelopes in Chinese

The Chinese way of addressing an envelope is different to that of the Western way. The receiver's address sits close to the top edge of the envelope, starting at the left hand corner as a token of respect, and is usually in one line. The receiver's name sits in the middle of the envelope. The sender's address sits close to the bottom edge of the envelope starting about midway as a token of humbleness, and is followed by the sender's name.

Writing a letter begins with the receiver's name or title followed by a colon. A greeting can follow the colon or at the start of the text. The text starts at the following line, two spaces in. The first line of every paragraph starts two spaces in, and there is no line space between paragraphs. To offer a wish at the end of the letter, the word "wish" takes a single line and starts four spaces in. Respectfully, the wish starts from the first space on the following line. The sender's name is then placed on the next line, but, humbly, at the right hand side. The letter then ends with the year and date next to the name on the following line.

谁的信

❀ Traditional food for festivals

元宵 yuánxiāo are ground sticky rice balls eaten during the Lantern Festival, 元宵节 Yuánxiāojié. They are about the size of a pingpong ball, 乒乓球 pīngpāngqiú, and are stuffed with sesame seed paste, bean paste or pork mince. They are boiled in soup seasoned with either sugar or salt, vegetables, and spices.

粽子 zòngzi is sticky rice wrapped with bamboo leaves eaten during the Dragon Boat Festival, 端午节 Duānwǔjié. There are two types – sweet, 碱粽 jiǎnzòng and meaty, 肉粽 ròuzòng. Jiǎnzòng is sticky rice mixed with baking soda and served with sugar or honey after cooking. Ròuzòng is sticky rice stuffed with seasoned pork, Chinese mushrooms and salty egg yolks. They are steamed or boiled.

元宵 yuánxiāo

粽子 zòngzi

月饼 yuèbǐng

月饼 yuèbǐng, moon cake, is eaten during the Mid-Autumn Festival, 中秋节 Zhōngqiūjié. There are also two types – one with flakey pastry and one Cantonese style. The flakey ones are stuffed with bean paste. The Cantonese ones are stuffed with bean paste, lotus seeds and salty egg yolks. Both are baked in the oven.

年糕 niángāo and 饺子 jiǎozi are both eaten during the Spring Festival, 春节 Chūnjié. Niángāo is eaten in southern China and jiǎozi in northern China. Niángāo is made of ground sticky rice sweetened with sugar. It is used to worship the god of the kitchen, 灶神 zàoshén, on the 23rd day of the last lunar month of the year. People hope that the god's mouth will be sweetened and will therefore say good words for them when he returns to heaven to report their deeds for the year. 饺子 Jiǎozi are dumplings stuffed with seasoned pork mince or seafood. Since it is shaped like a gold ingot, 元宝 yuánbǎo, as used in old China, it is eaten to symbolize the fortune of the coming year.

饺子 jiǎozi

元宝 yuánbǎo

灶神 zàoshén

dì shí kè fù xí
第十课 复习（二）

1 An entry in Xiaoming's blog

jì
中国旅行记

今年暑假的中国旅行，我们去了北京和西安，一共
          fēi   yú
玩了九天。大家都玩得非常愉快。

在北京的时候，我们买东西也买得很愉快。那儿的
                        shāng diàn
东西很便宜，我们什么都想买。在商店里，我们最喜欢
wèn   zhé
问 "打几折？" 和 "可以便宜一点儿吗？" 大伟还
      jiè
要向我借钱，他说他带的钱比我带的少。我没借他，因
为他买的东西比我买的多。

旅行的最后几天，很多人都感冒了。大伟又打喷嚏
ké sòu   hóu lóng   gài
又咳嗽。我也有点儿发烧，喉咙也疼。我想大概是因为
我们天天都太早起
chuáng   shuì
床，太晚睡觉了。

不过，回来后我

们的感冒都很

快就好了。

2 An entry in Dawei's blog

旅行的照片

今年九月的中国旅行是学校老师带我们去的，非^{fēi}常有意思。我们一共去了九天。

在北京，我们吃了很多好吃的，也买了不少东西。我看上了一部相机，可是我带的钱不多。小明带很多钱，我就向他借^{jiè}，可是他不借我，因为他想买的东西太多了。

我喜欢拍^{pāi}照。因为没有相机，我就用^{yòng}手机拍了很多长城和兵^{bīng}马俑^{yǒng}的照片。小明用^{yòng}他的相机也拍了不少照片。回来后，小明说他拍^{pāi}的照片比我拍的照片好看多了。兰兰比较客气，她说我拍的照片跟小明拍的一样好看。我当^{dāng}然^{rán}知道，相机拍^{pāi}的照片比较好，手机拍的照片比较差。

3 An entry in Lanlan's blog

吃胖一点儿

最近很多人病了。小明和大伟旅行回来，都感冒了。学校上课后，他们还请了一个星期的病假。

上上个星期，李秋感冒，请了两天病假。我吃坏了肚子，请了一天病假。上个星期，我也感冒了，发烧、喉咙疼、咳嗽，又请了三天病假。星期五我回学校上课，学校里人真少，因为很多同学和老师也都病了。我们班有三十个学生，可是只有十几个人去上课。

病了两次，我现在比以前苗条多了，可是同学们都说我太瘦了。大伟还买了蛋糕给我，说要我吃胖一点儿。

小明的生日会，他妈妈准备了很多好吃的东西。我们都吃得太多了。小明的生日礼物，我们都给他钱。小明说，他要用那些钱去买一个新的手机。我知道他已经看上了一个很好的手机。

4 **Language functions**

(6) Use of 比较 in comparison

他比较矮；我比较高。 Tā bǐjiào ǎi; wǒ bǐjiào gāo.

这件衣服比较小；那件比较大。 Zhè jiàn yīfu bǐjiào xiǎo; nà jiàn bǐjiào dà.

Use of 多了 in comparison

你高，他矮多了。 Nǐ gāo, tā ǎi duō le.

我的头发长，你的短多了。 Wǒ de tóufa cháng, nǐ de duǎn duō le.

Describing one's appearance using 长得

你姐姐长得很漂亮。 Nǐ jiějie zhǎng de hěn piàoliang.

他们俩儿长得很像。 Tāmen liǎr zhǎng de hěn xiàng.

Use of 比 in comparison

我爸爸比我胖。 Wǒ bàba bǐ wǒ pàng.

你的眼睛比我的大。 Nǐ de yǎnjing bǐ wǒ de dà.

Describing similarity using 跟 x 一样

她跟她妈妈一样漂亮。 Tā gēn tā māma yíyàng piàoliang.

他跟他爸爸一样高。 Tā gēn tā bàba yíyàng gāo.

(7) Asking about a plan

你打算暑假做什么？ Nǐ dǎsuàn shǔjià zuò shénme?

我打算去上海玩儿。 Wǒ dǎsuàn qù Shànghǎi wánr.

我打算去学钢琴。 Wǒ dǎsuàn qù xué gāngqín.

Asking about multiple destinations using 些

你们要去哪些地方？ Nǐmen yào qù nǎxiē dìfāng?

我们要去北京和西安。 Wǒmen yào qù Běijīng hé Xī'ān.

我们要去上海和桂林。 Wǒmen yào qù Shànghǎi hé Guìlín.

More uses of v + 过 for past experiences

你去过中国吗？ Nǐ qù guò Zhōngguó ma?

去过，我去过两次了。 Qù guò, wǒ qù guò liǎng cì le.

我没去过。 Wo méi qù guò.

Use of 好 to emphasize the completion of something

你们电影票买好了吗？ Nǐmen diànyǐng piào mǎi hǎo le ma?

我们已经买好了。 Wǒmen yǐjīng mǎi hǎo le.

还没，我们现在去买。 Hái méi, wǒmen xiànzài qù mǎi.

Use of 从……到

我从家里骑车到火车站。 Wǒ cóng jiāli qíchē dào huǒchēzhàn.

我们要从上海坐火车到北京。 Wǒmen yào cóng Shànghǎi zuò huǒchē dào Běijīng.

(8) Asking what happened using 怎么

> 你怎么了？ Nǐ zěnme le?
>
> 我觉得不太舒服。 Wǒ juéde bú tài shūfu.
>
> 我很好，没事啊！ Wǒ hěn hǎo, méi shì a!

Inquiring about someone's illness

> 你哪里不舒服？ Nǐ nǎli bù shūfu?
>
> 我肚子疼。 Wǒ dùzi téng.
>
> 我发烧、头疼。 Wǒ fāshāo, tóu téng.

Use of 可能 to state a probability

> 我看你可能感冒了。 Wǒ kàn nǐ kěnéng gǎnmào le.
>
> 我看我可能发烧了。 Wǒ kàn wǒ kěnéng fāshāo le.
>
> 他今天可能不来上课。 Tā jīntiān kěnéng bù lái shàngkè.

Use of 没 + v vs. 不 + v

> 他昨天没去学校，因为他病了。 Tā zuótiān méi qù xuéxiào, yīnwèi tā bìng le.
>
> 他昨天不去学校，因为他没做作业。 Tā zuótiān bú qù xuéxiào, yīnwèi tā méi zuò zuòyè.
>
> 弟弟明天不去学校。 Dìdi míngtiān bú qù xuéxiào.

Use of 次 to state frequency

> 一天三次，一次两粒。 Yì tiān sān cì, yí cì liǎng lì.
>
> 哥哥一个星期看两次电影。 Gēge yí gè xīngqī kàn liǎng cì diànyǐng.

Asking if someone is feeling better

> 你现在好点儿了吗？ Nǐ xiànzài hǎo diǎnr le ma?
>
> 我现在好多了，谢谢。 Wǒ xiànzài hǎo duō le, xièxie.
>
> 没有，还是很不舒服。 Méi yǒu, háishì hěn bù shūfu.

(9) Asking what present to give

> 你要送我什么礼物？ Nǐ yào sòng wǒ shénme lǐwù?
>
> 我要送你一本书。 Wǒ yào sòng nǐ yì běn shū.
>
> 我不知道，你想要什么？ Wǒ bù zhīdào, nǐ xiǎng yào shénme?

More use of 又

> 这件太大；那件又太小。 Zhè jiàn tài dà; nà jiàn yòu tài xiǎo.
>
> 这个我不喜欢；那个又太贵。 Zhè ge wǒ bù xǐhuān; nà ge yòu tài guì.

Use of v + 到

> 我们买到了音乐会的票。 Wǒmen mǎi dào le yīnyuèhuì de piào.
>
> 弟弟今天收到了很多礼物。 Dìdi jīntiān shōu dào le hěn duō lǐwù.

Use of 看上

> 他看上了那件很贵的衬衫。 Tā kànshàng le nà jiàn hěn guì de chènshān.
>
> 我知道你看上了我姐姐。 Wǒ zhīdào nǐ kànshàng le wǒ jiějie.

Appendix 1

WORDS AND EXPRESSIONS
Chinese-English

Simplified	Pinyin	English	Traditional	Lesson
A 矮	ǎi	*adj.* short (of stature); low (of houses, tables etc.)	矮	6
唉	ài	*exclaim.* (a sigh)	唉	1
爱	ài	*v.* love	愛	6
B 班	bān	*n.* class	班	2
班级	bānjí	*n.* class and grade	班級	1
办	bàn	*v.* handle, manage	辦	7
办公室	bàngōngshì	*n.* office	辦公室	3
帮	bāng	*v.* help, assist	幫	8
笨头笨脑	bèn tóu bèn nǎo	*adj.* stupid, have a thick skull	笨頭笨腦	6
比	bǐ	*prep.* (more) than; *v.* compare	比	6
比较	bǐjiào	*adv.* comparatively, relatively	比較	6
比赛	bǐsài	*n.* match, contest	比賽	4
兵马俑	Bīngmǎyǒng	*n.* Terracotta Warriors	兵馬俑	7
病	bìng	*adj.* sick; *n.* illness	病	8
病假	bìngjià	*n.* sick leave	病假	8
不过	búguò	*conj.* however, but	不過	7
不用	búyòng	*adv.* need not	不用	7
部	bù	*m.w.* [for films, cars etc.]; *n.* part	部	4
C 猜	cāi	*v.* guess	猜	1
餐	cān	*n.* meal	餐	6
参观	cānguān	*v.* visit	參觀	7
参加	cānjiā	*v.* attend, take part in	參加	7
操场	cāochǎng	*n.* sports ground	操場	3
差	chà	*adj.* not good, not up to standard; *v.* differ	差	1
差不多	chàbuduō	*adv.* approximately, nearly	差不多	3
长城	Chángchéng	*n.* the Great Wall	長城	7
长寿	chángshòu	*n.* long life, longevity	長壽	9
场	chǎng	*m.w.* [for shows, ball games etc.]; field, ground	場	4
唱	chàng	*v.* sing	唱	4
吃坏了肚子	chī huài le dùzi	*collq.* ate something bad that upset the stomach	吃壞了肚子	8
迟到	chídào	*v.* be late	遲到	2
出发	chūfā	*v.* set out, start off	出發	7
吹	chuī	*v.* play (flute, recorder etc.); blow	吹	4
春节	Chūnjié	*n.* Spring Festival, also called 新年 xīnnián in Taiwan (the beginning days of the lunar year)	春節	9
次	cì	*m.w.* [for frequency] time	次	4
聪明	cōngmíng	*adj.* clever, intelligent, bright	聰明	1
从	cóng	*prep.* from	從	7
D 打喷嚏	dǎ pēntì	*v.* sneeze	打噴嚏	8
打算	dǎsuàn	*v.* intend, plan; *n.* intention, plan	打算	7

Simplified	Pinyin	English	Traditional	Lesson
大雁塔	Dà Yàn Tǎ	*n.* Great Wild Goose Pagoda	大雁塔	7
担心	dānxīn	*v.* worry	擔心	7
当然	dāngrán	*adj.* of course, without doubt	當然	7
倒霉	dǎoméi	*v.* have bad luck	倒霉	8
到	dào	1. *v.* arrive, go to; 2. *prep.* to;	到	2, 3
		3. *suppl.* [used after a verb to indicate an achievement]		9
得	de	[used after a verb to indicate degree], e.g. 考得很好 - did the test very well	得	1
	dé	*v.* receive, get, e.g. 得十分 - received 10 marks		
	děi	*v.* have to, must		
笛子	dízi	*n.* flute	笛子	4
地点	dìdiǎn	*n.* place	地點	4
地方	dìfāng	*n.* place	地方	7
地理	dìlǐ	*n.* geography	地理	1
点儿	diǎnr	*adv.* a little, short for 一点儿	點兒	8
电视剧	diànshìjù	*n.* television drama	電視劇	4
电视迷	diànshìmí	*n.* television addict	電視迷	4
电视台	diànshìtái	*n.* television station	電視台	4
电影	diànyǐng	*n.* movie	電影	4
东	dōng	*n.* east	東	3
东京	Dōngjīng	*n.* Tokyo	東京	7
动画片儿	dònghuàpiānr	*n.* cartoon, also said as 动画片 dònghuàpiàn or 卡通片 kǎtōngpiàn	動畫片兒	4
肚子	dùzi	*n.* tummy, abdomen	肚子	8
肚子疼	dùzi téng/	*n.* stomachache; *v.* have a stomachache also said as 肚子痛 dùzi tòng	肚子疼	8
端午节	Duānwǔjié	*n.* Dragon Boat Festival	端午節	9
短裤	duǎnkù	*n.* shorts	短褲	7
短信	duǎnxìn	*n.* text message	短信	9
对	duì	*prep.* towards, to (regarding an attitude); *adj.* correct, right	對	4
对面	duìmiàn	*n.* opposite (location)	對面	3
多	duō	*adj.* 1. more than, over, e.g. 两千多 - more than two thousand; 一年多 - more than one year 2. many, much, e.g. 很多 - many/much *adv.* [indicating degree or extent] how, e.g. 多久 - how long (time duration)	多	2

E 二胡	èrhú	*n.* a two-stringed instrument played with a bow	二胡	4

F 发	fā	*v.* emit; send out;	發	8, 9
	fà	*n.* hair	髮	
发烧	fāshāo	*v.* have a temperature, run a fever	發燒	8
飞机	fēijī	*n.* airplane	飛機	7
分	fēn	*n.* mark; minute; cent	分	1

G 感冒	gǎnmào	*v.* have a cold; *n.* cold, flu;	感冒	8
钢琴	gāngqín	*n.* piano	鋼琴	4
高	gāo	*adj.* tall; high	高	6
高兴	gāoxìng	*adj.* happy, pleased	高興	10

Simplified	Pinyin	English	Traditional	Lesson
搞错	gǎocuò	*v.* make mistake, e.g. 你有没有搞错？- Are you out of your mind?	搞错	4
个性	gèxìng	*n.* personality	個性	6
个子	gèzi	*n.* stature, body build	個子	6
各有千秋	gè yǒu qiānqiū	*idiom.* each has its own merits	各有千秋	6
跟	gēn	*conj.* and	跟	6
功夫	gōngfū	*n.* kung fu, Chinese martial arts	功夫	4
公共汽车	gōnggòng qìchē	*n.* bus	公共汽車	3
公里	gōnglǐ	*n.* kilometer (km)	公里	3
古典	gǔdiǎn	*adj.* classical, e.g. 古典音乐 gǔdiǎn yīnyuè-classical music	古典	4
古典音乐	gǔdiǎn yīnyuè	*n.* classical music	古典音樂	4
古筝	gǔzhēng	*n.* a 21- or 25-stringed plucked instrument	古箏	4
拐	guǎi	*v.* turn	拐	3
管家婆	guǎnjiāpó	*n.* a nickname for house keeper	管家婆	6
桂林	Guìlín	*n.* a city in Guangxi, which is famous for its spectacular limestone scenery	桂林	7
过	guò	*v.* pass, cross	過	3
		par. [indicating a past experience]		4
过节	guòjié	*v.* celebrate festivals	過節	9
过夜	guòyè	*v.* spend the night, stay overnight	過夜	7

H 还可以	hái kěyǐ	*colloq.* not bad, OK	還可以	1
好好儿	hǎohāor	*adv.* to one's best, also said as 好好 hǎohǎo	好好兒	1
好久不见	hǎo jiǔ bú jiàn	*idiom.* long time no see	好久不見	6
嘿	hēi	*exclaim.* hey	嘿	2
红绿灯	hónglǜdēng	*n.* traffic light	紅綠燈	3
喉咙	hóulóng	*n.* throat, also said as 嗓子 sǎngzi	喉嚨	8
护照	hùzhào	*n.* passport	護照	7
回家	huíjiā	*v.* go home	回家	8
火车	huǒchē	*n.* train	火車	3
火车站	huǒchēzhàn	*n.* railway station	火車站	3

J 机场	jīchǎng	*n.* airport	機場	7
机票	jīpiào	*n.* airline ticket	機票	7
吉他	jítā	*n.* guitar	吉他	4
几	jǐ	*numeral.* a few; how many	幾	3
寄	jì	*v.* send, post, mail	寄	9
减肥	jiǎnféi	*v.* lose weight	減肥	6
健康	jiànkāng	*n.* health	健康	5
交	jiāo	*v.* hand in, e.g. 交作业 - hand in homework	交	2
教	jiāo	*v.* teach	教	4
饺子	jiǎozi	*n.* dumpling, in the shape of a gold ingot	餃子	9
教室	jiàoshì	*n.* classroom	教室	3
节	jié	*m.w.* [for lessons] section, period; *n.* festival	節	1
节目	jiémù	*n.* program	節目	4
借	jiè	*v.* lend; borrow	借	2
近	jìn	*adj.* near, close	近	3
京剧	jīngjù	*n.* Peking opera	京劇	4
久	jiǔ	*adj.* long (of time)	久	2

Simplified	Pinyin	English	Traditional	Lesson
就是	jiùshì	*adv.* just, simply (emphasizing a fact)	就是	1
旧金山	Jiùjīnshān	*n.* San Francisco	舊金山	7
卷	juǎn	*adj.* curly; *n.* roll	捲，卷	6
觉得	juéde	*v.* feel, think	覺得	6

K

Simplified	Pinyin	English	Traditional	Lesson
卡	kǎ	*n.* card, short for 卡片 kǎpiàn	卡	9
卡片	kǎpiàn	*n.* card, can be shortened as 卡 kǎ	卡片	9
卡通片	kǎtōngpiàn	*n.* cartoon, also said as 动画片	卡通	4
开	kāi	*v.* 1.hold (a meeting, exhibition etc.), e.g. 开生日会 - have a birthday party, 开音乐会 - have a concert; 2. open, start	開	9
开玩笑	kāi wánxiào	*v.* joke, make fun of	開玩笑	7
开夜车	kāi yèchē	*v.* study or work late into the night	開夜車	1
堪培拉	Kānpéilā	*n.* Canberra	堪培拉	7
看上	kànshàng	*v.* fancy, take a liking to	看上	9
考	kǎo	*v.* take/give an examination or a test	考	1
考试	kǎoshì	*n.* examination, test; *v.* take/give test	考試	1
科幻	kēhuàn	*n.* science fiction	科幻	4
科学	kēxué	*n.* science	科學	1
咳嗽	késòu	*v.* cough	咳嗽	8
可能	kěnéng	*adv.* maybe, probably	可能	8
可以	kěyǐ	*v.* may, can	可以	2
课	kè	*n.* subject, lesson	課	1
课本	kèběn	*n.* textbook	課本	2
课程表	kèchéng biǎo	*n.* school timetable	課程表	1
课业	kèyè	*n.* study, curriculum	課業	1

L

Simplified	Pinyin	English	Traditional	Lesson
拉	lā	*v.* play (violin, erhu etc.); pull	拉	4
拉肚子	lā dùzi	*v.* have diarrhoea	拉肚子	8
劳驾	láojià	[polite word used when asking for help] excuse me; may I trouble you	勞駕	3
离	lí	*adv.* away from	離	3
礼堂	lǐtáng	*n.* assembly hall, auditorium	禮堂	3
礼物	lǐwù	*n.* present, gift	禮物	9
粒	lì	*m.w.* [for small objects, e.g. tablets, buttons etc.]	粒	8
历史	lìshǐ	*n.* history	歷史	1
俩	liǎ	*colloq.* two (people), also said as 俩儿 liǎr	俩	6
流利	liúlì	*adj.* fluent	流利	2
路口	lùkǒu	*n.* intersection, crossing	路口	3
旅行	lǚxíng	*n. v.* travel	旅行	7
伦敦	Lúndūn	*n.* London	倫敦	3
啰唆	luōsuō	*adj.* long-winded	囉唆	9

M

Simplified	Pinyin	English	Traditional	Lesson
马虎	mǎhū	*adj.* careless, casual	馬虎	6
马路	mǎlù	*n.* road, street	馬路	3
马马虎虎	mǎmǎ hūhū	*colloq.* so-so; careless, casual	馬馬虎虎	2
没事	méishì	*adj.* alright, e.g. 你没事吧？ Are you alright? *v.* have no business, e.g. 我今天没事。 I am free today.	沒事	8
没意思	méi yìsi	*adj.* not interesting	沒意思	4
美	měi	*adj.* beautiful	美	7

Simplified	Pinyin	English	Traditional	Lesson
美术	měishù	*n.* the fine arts, art	美術	1
门票	ménpiào	*n.* entrance ticket	門票	4
迷	mí	*n.* enthusiast, fan, e.g. 电视迷 diànshìmí- television addict, 球迷 qiúmí- ball game fan	迷	4
迷路	mílù	*v.* lose one's way	迷路	7
免费	miǎnfèi	*v.* free of charge	免費	4
面	miàn	*n.* noodles, wheat flour	麵	9
苗条	miáotiáo	*adj.* (of a woman) slim	苗條	6
民歌	míngē	*n.* folk song, also called 民谣 mínyáo	民歌	4
民谣	mínyáo	*n.* folk song, also called 民歌 míngē	民謠	4
明陵	Míng Líng	*n.* Ming Tombs	明陵	7
墨尔本	Mò'ěrběn	*n.* Melbourne	墨爾本	7
N 拿来	ná lái	*v.* take (towards the speaker)	拿來	2
拿去	ná qù	*v.* take (away from the speaker)	拿去	2
南	nán	*n.* south	南	3
男	nán	*n.* man, male	男	2
男女合校	nán nǚ héxiào	*n.* co-educational school	男女合校	2
男子中学	nánzǐ zhōngxué	*n.* boy's middle/high school	男子中學	2
内向	nèixiàng	*adj.* introvert	內向	6
年糕	niángāo	*n.* New Year's cake, made of sticky rice flour	年糕	9
纽约	Niǔyuē	*n.* New York	紐約	3
女	nǚ	*n.* woman, female	女	2
女子中学	nǚzǐ zhōngxué	*n.* girl's middle/high school	女子中學	2
O 哦	ò	*exclaim.* [indicating understanding or realization]	哦	2
P 拍	pāi	*v.* take (photographs); clap (hands)	拍	7
旁边	pángbian	*n.* the side	旁邊	3
胖	pàng	*adj.* fat, plump	胖	6
票	piào	*n.* ticket	票	4
频道	píndào	*n.* (TV or radio) channel	頻道	4
Q 骑	qí	*v.* ride (bicycle or horse)	騎	3
奇怪	qíguài	*adj.* strange	奇怪	6
千	qiān	*n.* thousand	千	2
签证	qiānzhèng	*n.* visa	簽證	7
秦始皇	Qín Shǐhuáng	*n.* Qin Emperor	秦始皇	7
请	qǐng	*v.* 1. ask, e.g. 请假 qǐngjià- ask for leave; 2. please; 3. invite	請	8
请假	qǐngjià	*v.* to ask for leave	請假	8
庆祝	qìngzhù	*v.* celebrate	慶祝	9
球迷	qiúmí	*n.* ball game fan	球迷	4
球赛	qiúsài	*n.* ball game, match	球賽	4
区	qū	*n.* area, district	區	3
R 让	ràng	*v.* let, allow	讓	8
热门	rèmén	*n.* popular	熱門	4
热门音乐	rèmén yīnyuè	*n.* pop music	熱門音樂	4

Simplified	Pinyin	English	Traditional	Lesson
热闹	rènào	*adj.* lively, bustling with noise and excitement	熱鬧	9
认真	rènzhēn	*adj.* conscientious, earnest	認真	6
日记	rìjì	*n.* diary	日記	9
如果	rúguǒ	*conj.* if, in case, in the event of	如果	6
S 赛	sài	*n.* match, contest	賽	4
嗓子	sǎngzi	*n.* throat, also said as 喉咙 hóulóng	嗓子	8
上	shàng	*adj.* previous, upper e.g. 上一节 - previous lesson *v.* attend, go to, e.g. 上数学课 - attend maths lesson	上	1
上海	Shànghǎi	*n.* Shanghai, the largest city in China	上海	7
上课	shàngkè	*v.* attend lesson, go to class	上課	1
少	shǎo	*adv.* seldom; *adj.* few, little	少	8
生活	shēnghuó	*n.* life	生活	2
生日会	shēngrì huì	*n.* birthday party	生日會	9
十字路口	shízì lùkǒu	*n.* crossroads	十字路口	3
时间	shíjiān	*n.* time	時間	3
食品	shípǐn	*n.* food	食品	9
收	shōu	*v.* receive, collect	收	9
瘦	shòu	*adj.* 1. thin, lean; 2. tight (clothes fitting)	瘦	6
寿面	shòumiàn	*n.* birthday noodles	壽麵	9
暑假	shǔjià	*n.* summer vacation	暑假	7
数学	shùxué	*n.* mathematics	數學	1
水	shuǐ	*n.* water	水	8
睡过头	shuì guò tóu	*v.* sleep in accidentally	睡過頭	2
说曹操，曹操就到 shuō Cáo Cāo, Cáo Cāo jiù dào		speak of the devil. 曹操 (155-220 A.D.) was the ruler of Wei during the Age of the Three Kingdoms, known to be capable but crafty and evil.	說曹操，曹操就到	9
说话	shuōhuà	*v.* talk, speak	說話	2
送	sòng	*v.* give something as a present	送	9
随和	suíhé	*adj.* amiable, easy to get along with	隨和	6
T 塌	tā	*adj.* flat (nose); *v.* collapse	塌	6
台北	Táiběi	*n.* Taipei	台北	7
弹	tán	*v.* play (piano, guitar, guzheng etc.); spring, flick	彈	4
讨厌	tǎoyàn	*v.* hate	討厭	1
疼	téng	*v.* ache, also said as 痛 tòng	疼	8
体温	tǐwēn	*n.* body temperature	體溫	8
体育	tǐyù	*n.* physical education, sports	體育	1
天坛	Tiāntán	*n.* Temple of Heaven	天壇	7
天天	tiāntiān	*n.* every day	天天	3
挑剔	tiāoti	*v.* nitpick; *adj.* hypercritical	挑剔	6
挺	tǐng	*adj.* prominent (nose); *adv.* very	挺	6
痛	tòng	*v.* ache, also said as 疼 téng	痛	8
头脑	tóunǎo	*n.* brain	頭腦	1
头疼	tóuténg	*n.* headache; *v.* have a headache also said as 头痛 tóutòng	頭疼	8
图书馆	túshūguǎn	*n.* library	圖書館	3
W 哇	wa	*exclaim.* (amazed)	哇	1
外向	wàixiàng	*adj.* extrovert	外向	6

Simplified	Pinyin	English	Traditional	Lesson
玩儿	wánr	*v.* play, have fun	玩兒	7
晚餐	wǎncān	*n.* dinner	晚餐	6
晚会	wǎnhuì	*n.* evening entertainment	晚會	4
往	wǎng	*prep.* towards, to	往	3
忘	wàng	*v.* forget	忘	2
为什么	wèishénme	*adv.* why	為甚麼	1
文法学校	wénfǎ xuéxiào	*n.* grammar school	文法學校	2
问题	wèntí	*n.* question, problem	問題	2
卧虎藏龙	Wòhǔ Cánglóng	*n.* Crouching Tiger, Hidden Dragon, a popular Chinese kung fu movie	臥虎藏龍	4
无聊	wúliáo	*adj.* bored, boring	無聊	4
午餐	wǔcān	*n.* lunch	午餐	6
舞龙	wǔlóng	*n.* dragon dance	舞龍	4
舞狮	wǔshī	*n.* lion dance	舞獅	4

X

Simplified	Pinyin	English	Traditional	Lesson
西	xī	*n.* west	西	3
西安	Xī'ān	the capital city of Shaanxi (陕西 **Shǎnxī**) province where the entombed terracotta warriors were excavated	西安	7
西游记	Xīyóujì	*n.* Journey to the West, a Chinese classical novel telling the story of the Monkey King	西遊記	4
悉尼	Xīní	*n.* Sydney, also said as 雪梨 Xuělí	悉尼	3
细胞	xìbāo	*n.* cell (biological)	細胞	1
下	xià	*adj.* next; under	下	1
先	xiān	*adv.* first, in advance	先	8
香港	Xiānggǎng	*n.* Hong Kong	香港	7
相机	xiàngjī	*n.* camera	相機	7
向	xiàng	*prep.* to, towards (direction)	向	2
像	xiàng	*adj.* alike; *v.* be like, resemble	像	6
小卖部	xiǎomàibù	*n.* tuck shop, canteen	小賣部	3
小时	xiǎoshí	*n.* hour	小時	3
小提琴	xiǎotíqín	*n.* violin	小提琴	4
些	xiē	*m.w.* a few, some	些	7
新	xīn	*adj.* new	新	2
新年	xīnnián	*n.* Spring Festival, also called 春节 Chūnjié in China	新年	9
新闻	xīnwén	*n.* news	新聞	4
信	xìn	*n.* letter	信	5, 8
行	xíng	*v.* OK; to go	行	2
行程	xíngchéng	*n.* itinerary	行程	7
行李	xíngli	*n.* luggage, baggage	行李	7
兴趣	xìngqù	*n.* interest (in something)	興趣	4
姓名	xìngmíng	*n.* full name	姓名	1
休息	xiūxi	*v.* rest, take a rest	休息	8
休闲	xiūxián	*n.* leisure	休閒	4
嘘	xū	*colloq.* shh...	嘘	2
学习	xuéxí	*v.* study, learn	學習	2
雪梨	Xuělí	*n.* Sydney, also said as 悉尼 Xīní	雪梨	3

Y

Simplified	Pinyin	English	Traditional	Lesson
邀请	yāoqǐng	*v.* invite	邀請	9
药	yào	*n.* medicine	藥	8
一定	yídìng	*adv.* certainly	一定	9

Simplified	Pinyin	English	Traditional	Lesson
一样	yíyàng	*adj.* the same, equally	一樣	6
颐和园	Yíhé yuán	*n.* Summer Palace	頤和園	7
已经	yǐjīng	*adv.* already	已經	7
以后	yǐhòu	*adv.* later, after	以後	2
以前	yǐqián	*adv.* previously, before	以前	2
一点儿	yìdiǎnr	*adv.* a little, can be shortened as 点儿	一點兒	8
一起	yìqǐ	*adv.* together	一起	7
一天到晚	yìtiān-dàowǎn	*adv.* all day long, from morning till night	一天到晚	4
意思	yìsi	*n.* 1. meaning,	意思	2
		n. 2. fun, e.g. 有意思 - interesting		4
音乐会	yīnyuè huì	*n.* concert	音樂會	4
英俊	yīngjùn	*adj.* handsome	英俊	7
英语	Yīngyǔ	*n.* English	英語	1
用	Yòng	*v.* use	用	10
幽默感	yōumògǎn	*n.* sense of humor	幽默感	6
邮局	yóujú	*n.* post office	郵局	3
有线电视	yǒuxiàn diànshì	*n.* cable TV	有線電視	4
有意思	yǒu yìsi	*adj.* interesting	有意思	4
愉快	yúkuài	*adj.* happy, joyful	愉快	10
远	yuǎn	*adj.* far	遠	3
月饼	yuèbǐng	*n.* moon cake	月餅	9

Simplified	Pinyin	English	Traditional	Lesson
Z 糟糕	zāogāo	*exclaim.* oh no; how terrible	糟糕	2
早餐	zǎocān	*n.* breakfast	早餐	6
怎么	zěnme	*pro.* how, why	怎麼	1
站	zhàn	*n.* station; *v.* stand	站	3
张	zhāng	*m.w.* [for ticket, paper etc.]; *n.* Zhāng- a surname	張	4
长	zhǎng	*v.* grow; *adj.* cháng- long	長	6
照片	zhàopiàn	*n.* photograph	照片	7
真是的	zhēnshìde	*colloq.* a remark on something unpleasant	真是的	9
只	zhǐ	*adv.* only; [zhī- measure word for dogs, birds etc.]	只	1
钟	zhōng	*n.* clock, commonly added to 分 or 点, i.e. 三分钟 - three minutes; 三点钟 - three o'clock	鐘	3
中秋节	Zhōngqiūjié	*n.* Mid-Autumn Festival, also called Moon Festival (the 15th day of the eighth lunar month)	中秋節	9
周末	zhōumò	*n.* weekend	週末	4
住	zhù	*v.* live, reside	住	3
注意	zhùyì	*v.* pay attention to, take notice of	注意	2
准备	zhǔnbèi	*v.* prepare	準備	1
准时	zhǔnshí	*adj.* on time, punctual	準時	9
紫禁城	Zǐjìnchéng	*n.* the Forbidden City	紫禁城	7
自行车	zìxíngchē	*n.* bicycle, bike	自行車	3
粽子	zòngzi	*n.* dumplings made of sticky rice, wrapped in bamboo or reed leaves	粽子	9
走	zǒu	*v.* walk, go	走	3
走路	zǒulù	*v.* walk	走路	3
最近	zuìjìn	*n.* recently, lately	最近	8
作业	zuòyè	*n.* school assignment, homework	作業	2
做事	zuòshì	*v.* do things	做事	6

Appendix 2

WORDS AND EXPRESSIONS

English-Chinese

English	Simplified	Pinyin
A		
a few, some [*m.w.*]	些	xiē
a few; how many	几	jǐ
a little	(一)点儿	(yì)diǎnr
abdomen	肚子	dùzi
ache	疼 / 痛	téng / tòng
after	以后	yǐhòu
airline ticket	机票	jīpiào
airplane	飞机	fēijī
airport	机场	jīchǎng
alike, resemble	像	xiàng
all day long, from morning till night	一天到晚	yìtiān-dàowǎn
allow	让	ràng
already	已经	yǐjīng
alright	没事	méishì
(amazed) [*exclaim.*]	哇	wa
amiable	随和	suíhé
and	跟	gēn
approximately	差不多	chàbuduō
area, district	区	qū
arrive, go to	到	dào
art, the fine arts	美术	měishù
ask for leave	请假	qǐngjià
assembly hall	礼堂	lǐtáng
assist, help	帮	bāng
attend, go to	上	shàng
attend, take part in	参加	cānjiā
auditorium	礼堂	lǐtáng
away from	离	lí
B		
baggage, luggage	行李	xíngli
ball game	球赛	qiúsài
ball game fan	球迷	qiúmí
be like, resemble	像	xiàng
be late	迟到	chídào
beautiful	美	měi
before, previously	以前	yǐqián
bicycle	自行车	zìxíngchē
birthday noodles	寿面	shòumiàn
birthday party	生日会	shēngrìhuì
blow, play (flute etc.)	吹	chuī
body build, stature	个子	gèzi
body temperature	体温	tǐwēn
bored, boring	无聊	wúliáo
borrow	借	jiè
boy's middle/high school	男子中学	nánzǐ zhōngxué
brain	头脑	tóunǎo

English	Simplified	Pinyin
breakfast	早餐	zǎocān
bright, clever	聪明	cōngmíng
bus	公共汽车	gōnggòng qìchē
bustling with noise and excitement, lively	热闹	rènào
but, however	不过	búguò
C		
cable TV	有线电视	yǒuxiàn diànshì
camera	相机	xiàngjī
can, may	可以	kěyǐ
Canberra	堪培拉	Kānpéilā
canteen	小卖部	xiǎomàibù
card	卡(片)	kǎ(piàn)
careless, casual	马马虎虎	mǎmǎ hūhū
cartoon	动画片儿	dònghuàpiānr
	动画片	dònghuàpiàn
	卡通片	kǎtōngpiàn
celebrate	庆祝	qìngzhù
celebrate festivals	过节	guòjié
cell (biological)	细胞	xìbāo
cent; mark; minute	分	fēn
certainly	一定	yídìng
channel (TV or radio)	频道	píndào
Chinese martial arts, kung fu	功夫	gōngfū
Chinese musical instruments:		
1. a two-stringed instrument played with a bow	二胡	èrhú
2. a 21- or 25-stringed plucked instrument	古筝	gǔzhēng
class	班	bān
class and grade	班级	bānjí
classical	古典	gǔdiǎn
classical music	古典音乐	gǔdiǎn yīnyuè
classroom	教室	jiàoshì
clever	聪明	cōngmíng
clock, clock time	钟	zhōng
close, near	近	jìn
co-educational school	男女合校	nán nǚ héxiào
cold, flu	感冒	gǎnmào
collapse	塌	tā
collect	收	shōu
comparatively	比较	bǐjiào
compare	比	bǐ
concert	音乐会	yīnyuè huì
conscientious	认真	rènzhēn
contest	比赛 / 赛	bǐsài / sài
cough	咳嗽	késòu
cross, pass	过	guò

English	Simplified	Pinyin
crossing, intersection	路口	lùkǒu
crossroads	十字路口	shízì lùkǒu
Crouching Tiger, Hidden Dragon	卧虎藏龙	Wòhǔ Cánglóng
curly	卷	juǎn
curriculum, study	课业	kèyè

D

English	Simplified	Pinyin
definitely, certainly	一定	yídìng
diary	日记	rìjì
differ; not good	差	chà
dinner	晚餐	wǎncān
disease, illness	病	bìng
district, area	区	qū
do things	做事	zuòshì
Dragon Boat Festival	端午节	Duānwǔjié
dragon dance	舞龙	wǔlóng
dumpling, ingot shaped	饺子	jiǎozi
dumpling, in bamboo leaves	粽子	zòngzi

E

English	Simplified	Pinyin
each has its own merits	各有千秋	gè yǒu qiānqiū
earnest	认真	rènzhēn
east	东	dōng
easy to get along with	随和	suíhé
emit, send out	发	fā
English	英语	Yīngyǔ
enthusiast, fan	迷	mí
entrance ticket	门票	ménpiào
equally, the same	一样	yíyàng
evening entertainment	晚会	wǎnhuì
every day	天天	tiāntiān
examination	考试	kǎoshì
excuse me; may I trouble you	劳驾	láojià
extrovert	外向	wàixiàng

F

English	Simplified	Pinyin
fan, enthusiast	迷	mí
fancy, take a liking to	看上	kànshàng
far	远	yuǎn
fat, plump	胖	pàng
feel, think	觉得	juéde
female, woman	女	nǚ
festival	节	jié
few, little	少	shǎo
field, ground	场	chǎng
fine arts, art	美术	měishù
first, in advance	先	xiān
flat (nose)	塌	tā
flick, play (piano etc.)	弹	tán
flu, cold	感冒	gǎnmào
fluent	流利	liúlì
flute	笛子	dízi
folk song	民歌;	míngē;

English	Simplified	Pinyin
	民谣	mínyáo
food	食品	shípǐn
Forbidden City	紫禁城	Zǐjìnchéng
forget	忘	wàng
free of charge	免费	miǎnfèi
from	从	cóng
from morning till night	一天到晚	yìtiān-dàowǎn
full name	姓名	xìngmíng
fun, interest	意思	yìsi

G

English	Simplified	Pinyin
geography	地理	dìlǐ
get, receive	得	dé
gift	礼物	lǐwù
girl's middle/high school	女子中学	nǚzǐ zhōngxué
give sth. as a presentt	送	sòng
go home	回家	huíjiā
go, OK	行	xíng
go, walk	走	zǒu
go to, arrive	到	dào
go to, attend	上	shàng
go to class, have lesson	上课	shàngkè
grammar school	文法学校	wénfǎ xuéxiào
(The) Great Wall	长城	Chángchéng
Great Wild Goose Pagoda	大雁塔	Dà Yàn Tǎ
ground, field	场	chǎng
grow	长	zhǎng
guess	猜	cāi
guitar	吉他	jítā
Guilin, a city in Guangxi	桂林	Guìlín

H

English	Simplified	Pinyin
hair	头发	tóufa
hand in	交	jiāo
handle, manage	办	bàn
handsome	英俊	yīngjùn
happy, joyful	愉快	yúkuài
happy, pleased	高兴	gāoxìng
hate	讨厌	tǎoyàn
have a cold	感冒	gǎnmào
have a headache	头疼;	tóuténg;
	头痛	tóutòng
have a stomachache	肚子疼;	dùzi téng;
	肚子痛	dùzi tòng
have a temperature	发烧	fāshāo
have a thick skull, stupid	笨头笨脑	bèn tóu bèn nǎo
have bad luck	倒霉	dǎoméi
have diarrhoea	拉肚子	lā dùzi
have fun, play	玩儿	wánr
have lesson, go to class	上课	shàngkè
have no business, be free	没事	méishì
have to	得	děi
headache	头疼;	tóuténg;
	头痛	tóutòng

English	Simplified	Pinyin
health	健康	jiànkāng
help, assist	帮	bāng
hey	嘿	hēi
high, tall	高	gāo
history	历史	lìshǐ
hold, start	开	kāi
homework	作业	zuòyè
Hong Kong	香港	Xiānggǎng
hour	小时	xiǎoshí
house keeper (nickname)	管家婆	guǎnjiāpó
how, why	怎么	zěnme
how many; a few	几	jǐ
how terrible, oh no	糟糕	zāogāo
however	不过	búguò
hypercritical	挑剔	tiāoti

I

English	Simplified	Pinyin
if	如果	rúguǒ
ill, illness	病	bìng
in advance, first	先	xiān
in case, in the event of	如果	rúguǒ
[indicate an achievement]	到	dào
[indicate degree]	得	de
[indicate degree or extent] how	多	duō
[indicate realisation]	哦	ò
instruct, teach	教	jiāo
intend, to plan; intention	打算	dǎsuàn
interest (in something)	兴趣	xìngqù
interesting	有意思	yǒuyìsi
intersection	路口	lùkǒu
introvert	内向	nèixiàng
invite	邀请	yāoqǐng
invite, please	请	qǐng
itinerary	行程	xíngchéng

J

English	Simplified	Pinyin
joke (v.)	开玩笑	kāi wánxiào
just, simply	就是	jiùshì
Journey to the West	西游记	Xīyóujì
joyful	愉快	yúkuài

K

English	Simplified	Pinyin
kilometer (km)	公里	gōnglǐ
kung fu, Chinese martial arts	功夫	gōngfū

L

English	Simplified	Pinyin
lately, recently	最近	zuìjìn
later, after	以后	yǐhòu
lean, thin	瘦	shòu
learn, study	学习	xuéxí
leisure	休闲	xiūxián
lend	借	jiè
lesson, subject	课	kè

English	Simplified	Pinyin
let, allow	让	ràng
letter	信	xìn
library	图书馆	túshūguǎn
life	生活	shēnghuó
lion dance	舞狮	wǔshī
little, few	少	shǎo
live, reside	住	zhù
lively, bustling with noise	热闹	rènào
London	伦敦	Lúndūn
long (of time)	久	jiǔ
long life, longevity	长寿	chángshòu
long time no see	好久不见	hǎo jiǔ bú jiàn
long-winded	啰唆	luōsuō
lose one's way	迷路	mílù
lose weight	减肥	jiǎnféi
love (v.)	爱	ài
low (of houses, tables etc.)	矮	ǎi
luggage	行李	xíngli
lunch	午餐	wǔcān

M

English	Simplified	Pinyin
m.w. - lesson (period, section)	节	jié
m.w. - frequency (time)	次	cì
m.w. - show, ball game	场	chǎng
m.w. - birds, cats, dogs	只	zhī
m.w. - films, cars	部	bù
m.w. - paper, ticket (sheet)	张	zhāng
m.w. - tablets, buttons	粒	lì
mail (v.)	寄	jì
make fun of	开玩笑	kāi wánxiào
make mistake	搞错	gǎocuò
man, male	男	nán
manage, handle	办	bàn
many, much	多	duō
mark	分	fēn
match, contest	赛;	sài;
	比赛	bǐsài
mathematics	数学	shùxué
may, can	可以	kěyǐ
may I trouble you; excuse me	劳驾	láojià
maybe, probably	可能	kěnéng
meal	餐	cān
meaning	意思	yìsi
medicine	药	yào
Melbourne	墨尔本	Mò'ěrběn
Mid-Autumn Festival	中秋节	Zhōngqiūjié
Ming Tombs	明陵	Míng Líng
moon cake	月饼	yuèbǐng
Moon Festival	中秋节	Zhōngqiūjié
(more) than, compare	比	bǐ
more than, over	多	duō
movie	电影	diànyǐng
much, many	多	duō
must	得	děi

English	Simplified	Pinyin
N		
near	近	jìn
nearly, approximately	差不多	chàbuduō
need not	不用	búyòng
new	新	xīn
New Year's cake	年糕	niángāo
New York	纽约	Niǔyuē
news	新闻	xīnwén
next, under	下	xià
nickname for house keeper	管家婆	guǎnjiāpó
nitpick	挑剔	tiāoti
noodles	面	miàn
not bad, OK	还可以	hái kěyǐ
not good, not up to standard	差	chà
not interesting	没意思	méi yìsi
O		
of course	当然	dāngrán
office	办公室	bàngōngshì
oh no	糟糕	zāogāo
OK, not bad	还可以	hái kěyǐ
OK, alright	行	xíng
on time	准时	zhǔnshí
only	只	zhǐ
open, start	开	kāi
opposite (location)	对面	duìmiàn
over, more than	多	duō
P		
part, section	部	bù
pass, cross	过	guò
passport	护照	hùzhào
pay attention to	注意	zhùyì
Peking opera	京剧	jīngjù
personality	个性	gèxìng
photograph	照片	zhàopiàn
physical education	体育	tǐyù
piano	钢琴	gāngqín
place	地点;	dìdiǎn;
	地方	dìfāng
play, have fun	玩儿	wánr
plan, intend	打算	dǎsuàn
play (flute etc.); blow	吹	chuī
play (piano, guitar), flick	弹	tán
play (violin), pull	拉	lā
please, invite	请	qǐng
pleased, happy	高兴	gāoxìng
plump, fat	胖	pàng
pop music	热门音乐	rèmén yīnyuè
popular	热门	rèmén
post, send	寄	jì
post office	邮局	yóujú
prepare	准备	zhǔnbèi
present, gift	礼物	lǐwù

English	Simplified	Pinyin
previous, up	上	shàng
previously, before	以前	yǐqián
probably, maybe	可能	kěnéng
problem	问题	wèntí
program	节目	jiémù
prominent (nose)	挺	tǐng
pull, play (violin)	拉	lā
punctual	准时	zhǔnshí
Q		
Qin First Emperor	秦始皇	Qín Shǐhuáng
question	问题	wèntí
R		
railway station	火车站	huǒchēzhàn
receive, collect	收	shōu
receive, get	得	dé
recently	最近	zuìjìn
relatively, comparatively	比较	bǐjiào
(remark on something unpleasant)	真是的	zhēnshìde
resemble, alike	像	xiàng
reside	住	zhù
rest, take a rest	休息	xiūxi
ride (bicycle or horse)	骑	qí
road	马路	mǎlù
run a fever	发烧	fāshāo
S		
same, equally	一样	yíyàng
San Francisco	旧金山	Jiùjīnshān
school assignment	作业	zuòyè
school timetable	课程表	kèchéngbiǎo
science	科学	kēxué
science fiction	科幻	kēhuàn
section [m.w. for lessons]	节	jié
seldom, few, little	少	shǎo
send, post, mail	寄	jì
send out, emit	发	fā
sense of humor	幽默感	yōumògǎn
set out	出发	chūfā
Shanghai	上海	Shànghǎi
shh... (colloq.)	嘘	xū
short (of stature)	矮	ǎi
shorts	短裤	duǎnkù
sick, ill	病	bìng
sick leave	病假	bìngjià
side	旁边	pángbian
sigh (exclaim.)	唉	ài
simply, just	就是	jiùshì
sing	唱	chàng
sleep in accidentally	睡过头	shuì guò tóu
slim (of a woman)	苗条	miáotiáo
sneeze	打喷嚏	dǎ pēntì

English	Simplified	Pinyin
so-so	马马虎虎	mǎmǎ hūhū
some, a few [m.w.]	些	xiē
south	南	nán
speak, talk	说话	shuōhuà
speak of the devil	说曹操，曹操就到	shuō Cáo Cāo, Cáo Cāo jiù dào
spend the night	过夜	guòyè
sports, physical education	体育	tǐyù
sports ground	操场	cāochǎng
spring, play (piano, guitar)	弹	tán
Spring Festival	春节; 新年	Chūnjié; xīnnián
stand (v.), station	站	zhàn
start, hold	开	kāi
start off, set out	出发	chūfā
stature, body build	个子	gèzi
stomachache	肚子疼; 肚子痛	dùziténg; dùzitòng
strange	奇怪	qíguài
street, road	马路	mǎlù
study, curriculum	课业	kèyè
study, learn	学习	xuéxí
study late into the night	开夜车	kāi yèchē
stupid, have a thick skull	笨头笨脑	bèn tóu bèn nǎo
subject, lesson	课	kè
Summer Palace	颐和园	Yíhé yuán
summer vacation	暑假	shǔjià
Sydney	悉尼; 雪梨	Xīní; Xuělí

T

Taipei	台北	Táiběi
take (photographs)	拍	pāi
take (away)	拿去	ná qù
take (towards)	拿来	ná lái
take a liking to	看上	kànshàng
take a rest	休息	xiūxi
take a test or exam	考; 考试	kǎo; kǎoshì
take notice of	注意	zhùyì
take part in	参加	cānjiā
talk, speak	说话	shuōhuà
tall, high	高	gāo
teach, instruct	教	jiāo
television addict	电视迷	diànshìmí
television show	电视剧	diànshìjù
television station	电视台	diànshìtái
Temple of Heaven	天坛	Tiāntán
Terracotta Warriors	兵马俑	Bīngmǎyǒng
test, exam	考试	kǎoshì
text message	短信	duǎnxìn
textbook	课本	kèběn
thin, lean	瘦	shòu
think, feel	觉得	juéde

English	Simplified	Pinyin
thousand	千	qiān
throat	喉咙; 嗓子	hóulóng; sǎngzi
ticket	票	piào
time	时间	shíjiān
to one's best	好好; 好好儿	hǎohǎo; hǎohāor
together	一起	yìqǐ
Tokyo	东京	Dōngjīng
towards (attitude)	对	duì
towards (direction)	向; 往	xiàng; wǎng
traffic light	红绿灯	hónglùdēng
train	火车	huǒchē
travel	旅行	lǚxíng
tuck shop	小卖部	xiǎomàibù
tummy	肚子	dùzi
turn (direction)	拐	guǎi
two (people)	俩, 俩儿	liǎ, liǎr

U

under, next	下	xià
up, previous	上	shàng
upset stomach (by eating something bad)	吃坏了肚子	chī huài le dùzi

V

very, prominent (nose)	挺	tǐng
violin	小提琴	xiǎotíqín
visa	签证	qiānzhèng
visit (place, exhibition)	参观	cānguān

W

walk	走路	zǒulù
walk, go	走	zǒu
water	水	shuǐ
weekend	周末	zhōumò
west	西	xī
wheat flour, noodles	面	miàn
why	为什么	wèishénme
why, how	怎么	zěnme
without doubt, of course	当然	dāngrán
woman, female	女	nǚ
work late into the night	开夜车	kāi yèchē
worry	担心	dānxīn

X

Xi'an, capital city of Shaanxi province	西安	Xī'ān

130

Appendix 3

LIST OF RADICALS
部首目录

The first five radicals that only contain one stroke are also the five basic strokes in writing Chinese characters.
Their stroke names are: 横 héng (一); 竖 shù (丨); 撇 piě (丿); 点 diǎn (丶); 折 zhé (乙 乀 丁 乚).

① 一 yī one	丨 gǔn (down stroke)	丿 piě (left stroke)	丶 zhǔ (dot)	乙 乛乀乚 yǐ second (2nd)	② 十 shí ten	厂 hǎn cave	匚 fāng basket	卜 bǔ to predict
冂 jiōng borders	八 丷 bā eight	人 亻 rén people	勹 bāo to wrap	儿 rén people	匕 bǐ spoon	几 jī table	亠 tóu head	冫 bīng ice
宀 mì to cover	讠 yán to say, speech	凵 kǎn rice container	卩 巳 jié to control	阝 fù mound	阝 yì city	刀 刂 dāo knife	力 lì strength	厶 sī private
又 yòu also, again	廴 yǐn long walk	③ 干 gān shield	土 士 tǔ earth, soil	工 gōng work	艹 cǎo grass	寸 cùn inch; little	廾 gǒng to join hands	大 dà big
尢 兀 wāng lame	弋 yì to catch, take	小 ⺌ xiǎo little	口 kǒu mouth	囗 wéi to enclose	山 shān mountain	巾 jīn cloth	彳 chì left step	彡 shān hairy
夕 xì evening	夂 zhǐ to follow	饣 shí to eat; food	斗 qiáng plank	广 yǎn shelter	门 mén door	宀 mián large house	辶 chuò to go & stop	彐 ⺕ jì pig's head
尸 shī corpse	弓 gōng bow	己 jǐ self	子 zǐ child	屮 chè to burgeon	女 nǚ female	飞 fēi to fly	马 mǎ horse	纟 mì silk
幺 yāo little	巛 chuān river	④ 王 yù jade	无 wú not	韦 wéi leather	木 mù tree	支 zhī branch	犬 犭 quǎn dog	歹 dǎi evil
车 chē vehicle	牙 yá tooth	戈 gē spear	比 bǐ to compare	瓦 wǎ tile	止 zhǐ to stop	攴 攵 pū to tap	日 曰 rì sun	贝 bèi shell
水 氵 shuǐ water	见 jiàn to see	手 扌 ⺘ shǒu hand	牛 niú ox, cow	毛 máo hair	气 qì air	长 cháng long	片 piàn slice	斤 jīn axe
爪 爫 zhuǎ claw	父 fù father	月 yuè moon	氏 shì clan	风 fēng wind	欠 qiàn to owe	殳 shū a weapon	文 wén literature	方 fāng square

火 灬 huǒ fire	斗 dǒu a container	户 hù door	心 忄小 xīn heart	毋 母 wú do not	⑤示 礻 shì to notify	甘 gān sweet	石 shí stone	龙 lóng dragon
业 yè business	目 mù eye	田 tián field	罒 wǎng net	皿 mǐn plate	钅 jīn metal, gold	生 shēng to give birth	矢 shǐ arrow	禾 hé rice crop
白 bái white	瓜 guā melon	鸟 niǎo bird	疒 chuáng sickness	立 lì to stand	穴 xuè cave	疋 pǐ roll of cloth	皮 pí skin	癶 bō heel to heel
矛 máo spear	⑥耒 lěi plough	老 耂 lǎo old	耳 ěr ear	臣 chén officer	西 覀 yà to cover	而 ér also, but	页 yè page	至 zhì to
虍 hǔ tiger	虫 chóng insect	肉 ròu meat	缶 fǒu jar	舌 shé tongue	竹 ⺮ zhú bamboo	臼 jiù mortar	自 zì self, from	血 xiě blood
舟 zhōu boat	色 sè color	齐 qí even	衣 礻 yī clothes	羊 ⺶⺷ yáng sheep	米 mǐ rice	聿 ⺻ yù writing brush	艮 gèn tough	羽 yǔ feather
⑦麦 mài wheat	走 zǒu to walk	赤 chì red	豆 dòu bean	酉 yǒu wine	辰 chén time	豕 shǐ pig	卤 lǔ natural salt	里 lǐ village
足 ⻊ zú foot	身 shēn body	釆 biàn to separate	谷 gǔ valley	豸 zhì beast	龟 guī tortoise	角 jiǎo horn	辛 xīn bitter	⑧青 qīng green
卓 gàn morning sun	雨 yǔ rain	非 fēi not	齿 chǐ tooth	黾 mǐn toad	隹 zhuī short-tailed birds	鱼 yú fish	隶 lì slave	⑨革 gé leather
面 miàn face	韭 jiǔ garlic, chives	骨 gǔ bone	香 xiāng fragrant	鬼 guǐ ghost	音 yīn sound	首 shǒu head	⑩髟 biāo long hair	鬲 lì cauldron
鬥 dòu to fight	高 gāo tall, high	⑪黄 huáng yellow	麻 má hemp	鹿 lù deer	⑫鼎 dǐng tripod	黑 hēi black	黍 shǔ millet	⑬鼓 gǔ drum
鼠 shǔ rodent	⑭鼻 bí nose	⑰龠 yuè flute						

Appendix 4

CHARACTERS LEARNT IN 你好 1–3

(Characters learnt in this book are displayed in blue.)

Chinese (Radical)	Pinyin	English

1 Stroke

| 一（一） | yī | one (1-3) |

2 Strokes

二（一）	èr	two (1-3)
七（一）	qī	seven (1-3)
九（丿）	jiǔ	nine (1-3)
了（乙）	le	[grammatical word] (2-2)
十（十）	shí	ten (1-3)
八（八）	bā	eight (1-3)
人（人）	rén	people, person (1-1)
儿（儿）	ér	[word ending]; son (2-3)
几（儿）	jǐ	how many (1-4)
又（又）	yòu	and, again (3-9)

3 Strokes

三（一）	sān	three (1-3)
下（一）	xià	under, down (2-2)
久（丿）	jiǔ	long (of time) (3-2)
也（乙）	yě	also, too (1-8)
习（乙）	xí	to practise (3-2)
千（十）	qiān	thousand (3-2)
上（卜）	shàng	to go to, up (1-10)
个（人）	gè	[measure word] (1-6)
么（厶）	me	[word ending] (1-5)
大（大）	dà	big, large (1-7)
小（小）	xiǎo	little, small (1-7)
口（口）	kǒu	mouth (1-1)
山（山）	shān	mountain (1-1)
已（己）	yǐ	already (3-7)
子（子）	zi;	[word ending];
	zǐ	child (2-3)
女（女）	nǚ	woman, female (3-2)
飞（飞）	fēi	to fly (3-7)

Chinese (Radical)	Pinyin	English
马（马）	mǎ	horse (1-7)

4 Strokes

五（一）	wǔ	five (1-3)
开（一）	kāi	to open, to start, to hold (3-9)
不（一）	bù	no, not (1-5)
内（丨）	nèi	inside (3-6)
中（丨）	zhōng	center, middle (1-8)
为（丶）	wèi	for (2-8)
书（乛）	shū	book (2-2)
午（丿）	wǔ	noon, midday (2-2)
公（八）	gōng	public (3-3)
分（八）	fēn	minute; cent (2-2)
什（亻）	shén	what (1-5)
以（人）	yǐ	so as to (2-7)
今（人）	jīn	present (time) (2-1)
六（亠）	liù	six (1-3)
友（又）	yǒu	friend (1-10)
太（大）	tài	too, excessively (2-4)
天（大）	tiān	day; sky (2-1)
少（小）	shǎo	few, little (2-6), seldom (3-8)
车（车）	chē	car, vehicle (2-3)
比（比）	bǐ	to compare (3-4); (more) than (3-6)
日（日）	rì	day; sun (2-1)
水（水）	shuǐ	water (3-8)
见（见）	jiàn	to see (3-6)
手（手）	shǒu	hand (3-7)
毛（毛）	máo	10-cent unit; fur (2-6)
气（气）	qì	air (2-8)
长（长）	cháng	long (3-3)
	zhǎng	to grow (3-8)
片（片）	piān;	film (3-4);
	piàn	thin piece or slice (3-7)
月（月）	yuè	month; moon (2-1)
风（风）	fēng	wind (2-9)
方（方）	fāng	direction (3-7)

Chinese (Radical)	Pinyin	English
火 （火）	huǒ	fire *(3-3)*

5 Strokes

Chinese (Radical)	Pinyin	English
本 （木）	běn	[m.w. for books etc.] *(3-2)*
东 （一）	dōng	east *(3-3)*
平 （一）	píng	flat *(2-8)*
电 （丨）	diàn	electricity *(2-7)*
乐 （丿）	lè;	happy, joyful;
	yuè	music *(2-1)*
半 （丶）	bàn	half *(2-2)*
厌 （厂）	yàn	to detest *(3-1)*
他 （亻）	tā	he, him *(1-2)*
们 （亻）	men	[plural word] *(1-2)*
北 （丨）	běi	north *(2-9)*
写 （冖）	xiě	to write *(2-2)*
讨 （讠）	tǎo	to incur *(3-1)*
加 （力）	jiā	to add *(3-7)*
对 （又）	duì	right, correct *(2-1)*
		towards, to *(3-4)*
发 （又）	fā;	to emit, to send out;
	fà	hair *(3-8)*
去 （土）	qù	to go *(1-9)*
左 （工）	zuǒ	left (location) *(2-3)*
节 （艹）	jié	section; festival *(3-1)*
头 （大）	tóu	head *(3-8)*
只 （口）	zhī	[m.w. for some animals] *(1-7)*
	zhǐ	only *(3-1)*
右 （口）	yòu	right (location) *(2-3)*
可 （口）	kě	may, be permitted *(2-7)*
号 （口）	hào	date; number *(2-1)*
叫 （口）	jiào	to be called, to call *(1-10)*
四 （囗）	sì	four *(1-3)*
外 （夕）	wài	outside *(2-3)*
冬 （夂）	dōng	winter *(2-9)*
边 （辶）	biān	[word ending - location]; side *(2-3)*
末 （木）	mò	end *(3-4)*
汉 （氵）	hàn	name of a Chinese dynasty *(1-8)*
打 （扌）	dǎ	to hit, to play (tennis...etc.) *(1-9)*
		to dial (telephone) *(2-2)*
礼 （礻）	lǐ	courtesy, ritual *(3-9)*

Chinese (Radical)	Pinyin	English
业 （业）	yè	course of study *(3-2)*
生 （生）	shēng	to be born, to give birth to; pupil *(2-1)*
白 （白）	bái;	white;
	Bái	a surname *(2-4)*

6 Strokes

Chinese (Radical)	Pinyin	English
再 （一）	zài	again *(2-7)*
亚 （业）	yà	second *(1-8)*
年 （丿）	nián	year *(1-10)*
买 （一）	mǎi	to buy *(2-6)*
后 （厂）	hòu	behind, after *(2-3)*
同 （冂）	tóng	same; together *(1-10)*
共 （八）	gòng	together *(2-6)*
件 （亻）	jiàn	[m.w. for clothes] *(2-4)*
会 （人）	huì	to be able to, can *(1-8)*
先 （儿）	xiān	first *(2-4)*
交 （六）	jiāo	to hand in *(3-2)*
次 （冫）	cì	time (frequency) *(3-8)*
阴 （阝）	yīn	cloudy *(2-9)*
那 （阝）	nà	that *(1-5)*
动 （力）	dòng	to move *(1-9)*
欢 （又）	huān	happy *(1-9)*
地 （土）	dì	land, ground *(3-7)*
场 （土）	chǎng	field; [m.w. for shows] *(3-4)*
在 （土）	zài	[in progress]; at, in, on *(2-2)*
吗 （口）	ma	[question word] *(1-5)*
吃 （口）	chī	to eat *(1-11)*
向 （口）	xiàng	towards, to *(3-6)*
回 （囗）	huí	to return *(2-7)*
因 （囗）	yīn	cause *(2-8)*
岁 （山）	suì	year of age *(1-4)*
师 （巾）	shī	teacher *(1-4)*
行 （彳）	xíng	to go; OK *(3-3)*
多 （夕）	duō	many, much *(2-6)*
安 （宀）	ān	peace, peaceful *(3-7)*
字 （宀）	zì	character, word *(2-2)*
过 （辶）	guò	to pass, to cross *(3-3)*
好 （女）	hǎo	good, well *(1-2)*
她 （女）	tā	she, her *(1-4)*
妈 （女）	mā	mother *(1-6)*
如 （女）	rú	if *(3-6)*

Chinese (Radical)	Pinyin	English
红（纟）	hóng	red (2-4)
级（纟）	jí	grade, level (1-10)
机（木）	jī	machine (3-7)
收（攵）	shōu	to receive, to collect (3-9)
早（日）	zǎo	morning, early (2-2)
有（月）	yǒu	to have, there is/are (1-6)
百（白）	bǎi	hundred (3-2)
老（老）	lǎo	old (1-4)
考（老）	kǎo	to take/give a test (3-1)
西（西）	xī	west (3-3)
自（自）	zì	self (3-3)
色（色）	sè	color (2-4)
衣（衣）	yī	clothes (2-4)
米（米）	mǐ	uncooked rice (2-8)

7 Strokes

Chinese (Radical)	Pinyin	English
两（一）	liǎng	two (1-4)
来（一）	lái	to come (2-7)
更（一）	gèng	even, even more (2-6)
医（匚）	yī	doctor, medicine (3-8)
弟（丷）	dì	younger brother (1-6)
作（亻）	zuò	to do (3-2)
你（亻）	nǐ	you (1-2)
住（亻）	zhù	to live, to reside (3-3)
冷（冫）	lěng	cold (2-9)
别（刂）	bié	don't (3-4)
块（土）	kuài	dollar (oral) (2-6)
坏（土）	huài	bad, to go bad (3-8)
坐（土）	zuò	to sit, to board (3-3)
寿（寸）	shòu	longevity (3-9)
吧（口）	ba	[suggestion word] (1-9)
饭（饣）	fàn	cooked rice, meal (1-11)
间（门）	jiān	[m.w. for rooms] (2-3)
这（辶）	zhè	this (1-5)
还（辶）	hái	also, still (2-6)
运（辶）	yùn	to transport; luck (1-9)
迟（辶）	chí	late (3-1)
远（辶）	yuǎn	far (3-3)
近（辶）	jìn	near, close (3-3)
张（弓）	zhāng; Zhāng	[m.w. for paper]; a surname (3-4)
我（戈）	wǒ	I, me (1-2)

Chinese (Radical)	Pinyin	English
时（日）	shí	time, hour (2-7)
没（氵）	méi	[negative word] (1-7)
汽（氵）	qì	steam (3-3)
找（扌）	zhǎo	to look for; to give change (2-7)
肚（月）	dù	abdomen (3-8)
忘（心）	wàng	to forget (3-2)
快（忄）	kuài	fast; soon (2-1); be quick (3-8)
男（田）	nán	man, male (3-2)
利（禾）	lì	sharp (1-8)
走（走）	zǒu	to walk, to go (3-3)
里（里）	lǐ	inside (2-3)

8 Strokes

Chinese (Radical)	Pinyin	English
事（一）	shì	matter, thing, business (2-7)
果（木）	guǒ	fruit; result (3-6)
卖（十）	mài	to sell (2-6)
周（冂）	zhōu	week (3-4)
京（亠）	jīng	capital (2-9)
话（讠）	huà	speech (2-7)
试（讠）	shì	test, to try (3-1)
参（厶）	cān	to participate (3-7)
英（艹）	yīng	brave, elite (1-8)
呢（口）	ne	[question word] (2-3)
国（囗）	guó	nation, country (1-8)
往（彳）	wǎng	towards, to (3-3)
备（田）	bèi	to prepare (3-1)
空（宀）	kòng	free time, spare time (2-7)
宜（宀）	yí	suitable (2-6)
宠（宀）	chǒng	to spoil (1-7)
学（子）	xué	to study, to learn (1-10)
姐（女）	jiě	elder sister (1-6)
妹（女）	mèi	younger sister (1-6)
经（纟）	jīng	to pass through (3-7)
玩（王）	wán	to play, to have fun (3-7)
现（王）	xiàn	now, present (2-2)
狗（犭）	gǒu	dog (1-7)
些（止）	xiē	[m.w.] a few, some (3-7)
明（日）	míng	bright (light) (2-1)
物（牛）	wù	object, thing (1-7)
爸（父）	bà	father (1-6)
服（月）	fú	clothes (2-4)
朋（月）	péng	friend (1-10)

Chinese (Radical)	Pinyin	English
所（户／斤）	suǒ	so; place (2-8)
炒（火）	chǎo	to stir-fry (2-8)
性（忄）	xìng	nature, character (3-6)
视（礻）	shì	sight; to look at (3-4)
知（矢）	zhī	to know (3-1)
和（禾）	hé	and, with (1-10)
的（白）	de	[possessive particle] (1-5)
到（至）	dào	to arrive, to go to; to (3-2)
房（方）	fáng	room, house (2-3)
雨（雨）	yǔ	rain (2-9)

9 Strokes

Chinese (Radical)	Pinyin	English
南（十）	nán	south (3-3)
点（灬）	diǎn	o'clock; dot; to point (2-2)
前（丷）	qián	front, before (2-3)
便（亻）	pián; biàn	cheap; convenience (2-6)
信（亻）	xìn	letter (mail) (3-9)
说（讠）	shuō	to speak, to say (1-8)
语（讠）	yǔ	language (1-8)
城（土）	chéng	town (2-8)
茶（艹）	chá	tea (2-8)
药（艹）	yào	medicine (3-8)
哪（口）	nǎ	where; which; what (2-3)
带（巾）	dài	to take, bring (3-7)
很（彳）	hěn	very (1-7)
饼（饣）	bǐng	biscuit, cake (3-9)
饺（饣）	jiǎo	dumpling (gold ingot-shaped) (3-9)
穿（穴）	chuān	to wear (2-4)
客（宀）	kè	guest (2-8)
送（辶）	sòng	to give sth. as a present; escort (3-9)
迷（辶）	mí	fan; to lose one's way (3-4)
给（纟）	gěi	to give (2-6)
相（木）	xiàng	appearance, photo (3-7)
是（日）	shì	is, am, are (1-2)
昨（日）	zuó	yesterday (2-1)
星（日）	xīng	star (2-1)
春（日）	chūn	spring (2-9)
冒（冖）	mào	to emit, to risk (3-8)
贵（贝）	guì	expensive, dear (2-6)
觉（见）	jué; jiào	to feel; sleep (3-6)
看（手）	kàn	to read, to see, to watch (2-2)

Chinese (Radical)	Pinyin	English
胖（月）	pàng	fat, plump (3-6)
怎（心）	zěn	how (2-4)
祝（礻）	zhù	to wish (offer good wishes) (2-1)
思（田）	sī	to think (3-4)
科（禾）	kē	science (3-1)
秋（禾）	qiū	autumn, fall (2-9)
要（西）	yào	to want, would like (2-6)
差（羊）	chà	not good (3-1); differ (3-3)
面（面）	miàn	[word ending - location]; face (2-3); noodles, wheat flour (3-9)
音（音）	yīn	sound (3-4)

10 Strokes

Chinese (Radical)	Pinyin	English
哥（一）	gē	elder brother (1-6)
真（十）	zhēn	really (1-11)
候（亻）	hòu	time (2-7)
高（高）	gāo	tall; high (3-6)
离（亠）	lí	away from (3-3)
凉（冫）	liáng	cool (2-9)
准（冫）	zhǔn	standard (3-1)
课（讠）	kè	lesson, subject (3-1)
请（讠）	qǐng	please; to invite (2-7)
谁（讠）	shéi	who, whom (1-4)
部（阝）	bù	[m.w. for films]; part (3-4)
都（阝）	dōu	all (2-8)
能（厶）	néng	can, to be able to (3-8)
夏（夂）	xià	summer (2-9)
饿（饣）	è	hungry (1-11)
家（宀）	jiā	family, home (1-6)
班（王）	bān	class (3-2)
校（木）	xiào	school (3-2)
样（木）	yàng	appearance (2-4)
较（车）	jiào	to compare; relatively (3-6)
旅（方）	lǚ	to travel (3-7)
热（灬）	rè	hot (2-9)
烧（火）	shāo	to burn (3-8)
钱（钅）	qián	money (2-6)
疼（疒）	téng	to ache (3-8)
病（疒）	bìng	sick, illness (3-8)
站（立）	zhàn	station, stop; to stand (3-3)
起（走）	qǐ	to rise, to get up (3-9)

Chinese	Pinyin	English

11 Strokes

Chinese	Pinyin	English
假 (亻)	jià	holiday; leave of absence *(3-7)*
做 (亻)	zuò	to do, to make *(2-2)*
菜 (艹)	cài	dish, vegetable *(1-11)*
常 (丷)	cháng	often *(2-8)*
得 (彳)	de	[degree, result of] *(2-8)*
	dé	to receive, to get *(3-1)*
	děi	have to, must *(3-1)*
馆 (饣)	guǎn	building *(2-8)*
寄 (宀)	jì	to send, to post, to mail *(3-9)*
骑 (马)	qí	to ride (bicycle or horse) *(3-3)*
绿 (纟)	lù	green *(2-4)*
球 (王)	qiú	ball *(1-9)*
晚 (日)	wǎn	evening, late *(2-2)*
您 (心)	nín	you [polite form] *(2-7)*
蛋 (疋)	dàn	egg *(3-9)*
票 (覀)	piào	ticket *(3-4)*
第 (⺮)	dì	(order) *(3-1)*
雪 (雨)	xuě	snow *(2-9)*
黄 (黄)	huáng	yellow;
	Huáng	a surname *(2-4)*

12 Strokes

Chinese	Pinyin	English
舒 (人)	shū	comfortable *(3-8)*
就 (一)	jiù	merely; then, therefore *(3-1)*
谢 (讠)	xiè	to thank *(2-8)*
喜 (士)	xǐ	to like; happy *(1-9)*
喝 (口)	hē	to drink *(1-11)*
道 (辶)	dào	way *(3-1)*
晴 (日)	qíng	sunny, fine *(2-9)*
暑 (日)	shǔ	heat, hot weather *(3-7)*
最 (日)	zuì	the most *(2-9)*
渴 (氵)	kě	thirsty *(1-11)*
期 (月)	qī	a period of time *(2-1)*
短 (矢)	duǎn	short (length) *(3-6)*
等 (⺮)	děng	to wait *(2-7)*
黑 (黑)	hēi	black *(2-4)*

13 Strokes

Chinese	Pinyin	English
像 (亻)	xiàng	alike; to resemble *(3-6)*

Chinese	Pinyin	English
蓝 (艹)	lán	blue *(2-4)*
数 (攵)	shù	numbers *(3-1)*
照 (灬)	zhào	to take (photos), photo *(3-7)*
感 (心)	gǎn	to feel, sense *(3-8)*
想 (心)	xiǎng	to think *(1-11)*
错 (钅)	cuò	wrong, incorrect *(2-1)*
矮 (矢)	ǎi	short (height), low (height) *(3-6)*
意 (立)	yì	meaning *(3-4)*
跟 (足)	gēn	and *(3-6)*
路 (足)	lù	road *(3-3)*

14 Strokes

Chinese	Pinyin	English
赛 (宀)	sài	match, contest *(3-4)*
瘦 (疒)	shòu	thin, lean; tight (fitting) *(3-6)*
端 (立)	duān	up right *(3-9)*
算 (⺮)	suàn	to calculate *(3-7)*
粽 (米)	zòng	dumpling (in bamboo leaves) *(3-9)*

15 Strokes

Chinese	Pinyin	English
影 (彡)	yǐng	movie, shadow, image *(3-4)*
澳 (氵)	ào	bay *(1-8)*

16 Strokes

Chinese	Pinyin	English
糕 (米)	gāo	cake, pudding *(3-9)*

Answers:

p. 36 – 你猜是什么？
   影像 reflection

p. 68 – 谁高？
   黄蓝最高，高明最矮。

p. 92 – 你知道吗？
   他是医生。

Appendix 5

LEARN TO WRITE

by lesson

Chinese		English
1 第	dì	(order)
课	kè	lesson, subject
数	shù	numbers
科	kē	science
知	zhī	to know
道	dào	way
节	jié	section; festival
讨	tǎo	to incur
厌	yàn	to detest
就	jiù	merely; then, therefore
考	kǎo	to take/give a test
试	shì	test, to try
差	chà	not good; differ
准	zhǔn	standard
备	bèi	to prepare
2 班	bān	class
校	xiào	school
女	nǚ	woman, female
男	nán	man, male
千	qiān	thousand
百	bǎi	hundred
习	xí	to practise
久	jiǔ	long (of time)
本	běn	[m.w. for books etc.]
作	zuò	to do
业	yè	course of study
忘	wàng	to forget
迟	chí	late
到	dào	to go to, to arrive; to
交	jiāo	to hand in
3 走	zǒu	to walk, to go

Chinese		English
路	lù	road
骑	qí	to ride (bicycle or horse)
自	zì	self
行	xíng	to go; OK
坐	zuò	to sit, to board
火	huǒ	fire
公	gōng	public
汽	qì	steam
长	cháng;	long
	zhǎng	to grow
住	zhù	to live, to reside
东	dōng	east
西	xī	west
南	nán	south
离	lí	away from
远	yuǎn	far
近	jìn	near, close
往	wǎng	towards, to
站	zhàn	station; to stand
过	guò	to pass, to cross
4 视	shì	sight, to look at
部	bù	[m.w. for films]; part
意	yì	meaning
思	sī	to think
场	chǎng	[m.w. for shows]; field
比	bǐ	to compare; (more) than
赛	sài	match, contest
别	bié	don't
迷	mí	fan; to lose one's way
周	zhōu	week
末	mò	end
影	yǐng	movie, shadow

Chinese		English		Chinese		English
张	zhāng;	[m.w. for paper];		机	jī	machine
	Zhāng	a surname		已	yǐ	already
票	piào	ticket		经	jīng	to pass through
音	yīn	sound		手	shǒu	hand
				飞	fēi	to fly

6

见	jiàn	to see
像	xiàng	alike, to resemble
较	jiào	to compare, relatively
高	gāo	tall; high
矮	ǎi	short (height), low (height)
觉	jué; jiào	to feel; sleep
短	duǎn	short (length)
瘦	shòu	thin, lean; tight (fitting)
胖	pàng	fat, plump
如	rú	if
果	guǒ	fruit; result
跟	gēn	and
性	xìng	nature, character
内	nèi	inside
向	xiàng	towards, to

8

病	bìng	sick, illness
舒	shū	comfortable
头	tóu	head
疼	téng	to ache
发	fā; fà	to emit, to send out; hair
烧	shāo	to burn
能	néng	can, to be able to
感	gǎn	to feel, sense
冒	mào	to emit, to risk
肚	dù	abdomen
医	yī	doctor, medicine
坏	huài	bad; to go bad
药	yào	medicine
次	cì	time (frequency)
水	shuǐ	water

7

旅	lǚ	to travel
算	suàn	to calculate
暑	shǔ	heat, hot weather
假	jià	holiday; leave of absence
参	cān	to participate
加	jiā	to add
些	xiē	m.w. a few, some
地	dì	land, ground
方	fāng	direction
安	ān	peace, peaceful
玩	wán	to play, to have fun
照	zhào	to take (photos); photo
片	piàn;	thin piece or slice;
	piān	film
带	dài	to take, to bring
相	xiàng	appearance, photo

9

开	kāi	to hold, to open, to start
寄	jì	to send, to post, to mail
起	qǐ	to rise, to get up
收	shōu	to receive, to collect
信	xìn	letter (mail)
礼	lǐ	courtesy, ritual
送	sòng	to give sth. as a present
又	yòu	and, again
寿	shòu	longevity
蛋	dàn	egg
糕	gāo	cake, pudding
端	duān	up right
粽	zòng	dumpling (in bamboo leaves)
饼	bǐng	biscuit, cake
饺	jiǎo	dumpling (gold ingot-shaped)